The
Little System 7.1/7.5
Book

Kay Yarborough Nelson

Peachpit Press
Berkeley, California

The Little System 7.1/7.5 Book
Kay Yarborough Nelson

Peachpit Press
2414 Sixth Street
Berkeley, CA 94710
510/548-4393
510/548-5991 (fax)

Peachpit Press is a division of Addison-Wesley Publishing Company.

Cover Design: **TMA** Ted Mader Associates

ISBN: 1-56609-151-9

0 9 8 7 6 5 4 3 2

♻ Printed on Recycled Paper

Printed and bound in the United States of America

Magic loose in the world.
It was as good an explanation as any...

— Robert A. Heinlein, *Waldo & Magic, Inc.*

Contents

Introduction

You may still be running System 7, and that's OK! This book is about System 7 in general—System 7.1 and 7.5 just added a few more features to System 7. So "System 7" means "System 7, System 7.1, and sometimes System 7.5" here (the new stuff for System 7.5 is in Chapters 11 and 12). If there's something brand-new in System 7.1, there's usually a tip in the margin about it. So you're cool, with any System 7.X and this little book. In fact, a few of you may still be running System 6 and looking in this book to see what 7 is all about. If that's the case, you'll be glad to know that it has tips for mixing Systems 6 and 7, too.

At the time of this writing (mid-1994), Apple estimates that the great majority of us Mac users have switched to System 7. There's no reason to wait any longer. Software is being developed for System 7 only. And in fact, System 7 is just a lot more fun than System 6. If you've got a Mac with 4 megs of memory (let's be honest here: Apple says you need 2 megs but you and I know you need 4), you're ready for System 7. You will *need* 4 megs for 7.5; 8 megs if you want PowerTalk and QuickDraw GX. (More if you have a PowerMac.)

This *Little System 7.1/7.5 Book* assumes that you know about basic Mac operations, like using a mouse for clicking, double-clicking, dragging, and things like that. If you go through Chapters 2 and 3, you'll see that the basics are covered at a pretty fast clip. Chapter 1 is a preview of the features that are new in System 7, with page references to where each new feature is discussed in the rest of the book.

◀ **Tip:** *The Performa series comes with a stripped-down version of System 7.X, called System 7.XP, already installed. It's designed to be super easy and safe to use. For example, an Application Launcher lets you start programs with one click. When you outgrow the Performa's system, you can install System 7.1 or System 7.5 over it.*

If you already know about System 7.1 and you're interested in what's in System 7.5, start at the back of the book, in Chapter 11. System 7.5 works *just like* System 7.1: it just gives you more goodies and control panels. So what you know is still true, and all you have to do is go exploring to see which of the new stuff you want to keep. (There's a lot of new control panels and extensions, and you may not want them all.)

Still with System 7.0?

System 7.5 brings you copying by drag and drop between applications (applications that support it, that is), a new interactive Help system, roll-up windows, hierarchical Apple menus, scripting in the Finder (this is cool), Sticky Memos (Post-It notes), a better Finder, SuperClock, SimpleText, an improved Note Pad and Scrapbook, a Finder you can configure to work like a Performa (easier for new users), Macintosh PC Exchange and Easy Open for exchanging DOS/Windows documents, and all kinds of new control panels: Apple Menu Options for keeping track of what you looked at last, Auto Power On/Off, Date & Time, Desktop Patterns, Extensions Manager, MacTCP for the Internet, Network, Sound, Text, Monitors... these are just a few of the new or improved control panels. There's all sorts of stuff for PowerBook users, too, including a new Control Strip that makes trips to the control panels less frequent.

What's New in System 7.1?

If you have 8 megs of RAM or more, you can also install PowerTalk and QuickDraw GX after you install System 7.5. (PowerMacs need 16 megs of RAM for these extras, and 8 megs just for System 7.5.) PowerTalk is Apple's new collaboration software with the universal mailbox, and QuickDraw GX is the next generation of printing technology. These new features are covered in Chapter 12.

Many Thanks

In case you're interested (this stymied at least one reviewer), PorkChop is a cat. He's a plump little bobtail. He's still here for the third edition, as is Pusser (Pussmaster General) the PowerBook.

And many thanks, as always, to Matt Kim for page makeup.

What's New in System 7?

This chapter's primarily so that you can quickly see what System 7's new features are. You'll find more information about each new feature and how you use it if you look up the page reference.

New features crop up all over the place in System 7, not just where you might logically expect them to be. This chapter gives you an overview and directs you to where each new feature's discussed later in the book.

◀ Tip: *System 7.5's additional features are covered starting on p. 139.*

The most obvious new feature of System 7 is the way the Finder looks and acts. When you're looking at any view except icons, you'll see folders, just like always, but they'll have tiny triangles next to them. Click on a triangle, and the view expands to show you what's in the folder in outline form, instead of opening a new window.

The Finder's New Look and Feel

◀ Tip: *System 7.5's Finder is scriptable—you can use a macro recorder with it to carry out a set of operations.*

```
▽  🗀 System Folder ———————— Expanded folder
▷       🗀 Apple Menu Items
        🗋 Clipboard  ———— Collapsed folder
▷       🗀 Control Panels
▷       🗀 Extensions
        🗋 Finder
▷       🗀 Preferences
        🗋 Scrapbook File
▷       🗀 Startup Items
        🗋 System
```

◀ Tip: *Use the View menu to choose different ways to look at things.*

These are called **outline views**, and they let you hunt for files without opening a whole bunch of windows on your desktop. They make copying and moving files from folder to folder a lot easier, too. See page 13.

Changing Names

When you click on a name to change it, System 7 very conveniently puts a box around it, so that you know you can go ahead and type a new name instead of selecting an icon and then starting to type and renaming it by mistake. See page 37.

Multitasking

Multitasking's built into System 7: you can work with more than one program at a time and jump back and forth between them without quitting from one and opening another. The little icon in the upper-right corner of your screen is the **Application menu**. It shows you which program is active. Clicking on it shows you all the programs you've got running. You can choose the one you want from this list to switch to it, or click in the window of the one you want to make it active. You can hide all the windows except the one for the program you're in, or show all the windows of everything you've got running. See pages 16, 58.

▶ **Tip:** *You can continue to work in a program while files are being copied, too.*

Finder Shortcuts

There are new shortcuts for navigating through what's in a window, ones that old Mac hands have longed for. Typing the first few letters of an icon's name will select it. Also, pressing the arrow keys will move you from icon to icon. And if you have an extended keyboard, the PgUp, PgDn, Home, and End keys will zip you through Finder windows. See page 18.

▶ **Tip:** *Just type the first few letters of something's name to move straight to it.*

Scrolling's improved a lot, too. In a list view, you can drag an item to a window border, and the window will scroll to show you what's in it. When you release the mouse button, the item pops back to where you picked it up. Or you can scroll with the arrow keys; just hold 'em down. See page 17.

More new **Finder tricks**: To see where you are in the filing hierarchy, Command-click in the window's title. (The Command key's the one that looks like a cloverleaf: ⌘) See page 14.

To sort a Finder window alphabetically (unless you're looking at icons), click on Name. To sort it by Size, click on Size. You get the idea.

To sort icons alphabetically, press the Option key and choose Clean Up by Name from the Special menu.

There are all sorts of new **keyboard shortcuts**. Some folks hate 'em and would rather mouse around, and some love 'em. All I can say is do what comes naturally. For example, when you're looking at outline views, Command-Right arrow will expand the outline, and Command-Left arrow will collapse it again.

To see more new Finder keyboard shortcuts, click on the Help icon (it's the one with the question mark in the upper-right corner of your screen) and choose (you guessed it) Finder Shortcuts. See page 22.

Balloon Help

You can choose **Show Balloons** from the ? (Help) menu, and the Mac will show you a balloon that tells about each item that you drag the pointer over.

Software developers are putting balloons in their new products, too, so you can find out what strange new icons are for and explore new commands in the programs you buy.

Balloon Help is useful for the first few minutes you're working with System 7 or a new program, but it gets old in a hurry, because the balloons hide what you're looking at. You'll probably want to Hide Balloons pretty soon.

▶ **Tip:** *With System 7.5, you can have a Launcher and a Documents folder in your Finder, just like on a Performa, to make the Finder easier for new users.*

◀ **Tip:** *To open the window that holds the active window, press Command-Up arrow. To open a folder into a new window, press Command-Down arrow (or just double-click on it).*

◀ **Tip:** *You can use your Mac while it's showing balloons. Everything still works fine, even though you can't see it all.*

◀ **Tip:** *System 7.5 comes with new interactive help called Macintosh Guide. You use it by choosing it from the Help menu.*

The Trash

Trash Trash

With System 7, the **Trash** isn't emptied until you empty it. You also have to confirm that you really want to empty the Trash. Whatever you put in the Trash will stay there, even if you turn off your computer. You can't put the blame on the trash can any more for throwing out your files. Page 40.

The New Desktop

The **Desktop** is now recognized as a real place instead of as an invisible file, like it was before: it's at the very top of your filing system, and you can get there from a standard directory dialog box when you use the Open or Save As command. You don't have to use a Drive button to switch disk drives when you want to select something on another disk; you just choose the disk from the Desktop's contents. See page 61.

You clicked here to go to the desktop

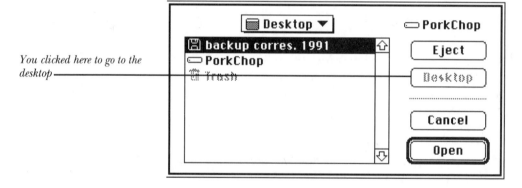

Opening Documents

There's a new way to open documents, too: you can open a document by dragging its icon onto a program's icon. If the program can open that document, it will. This lets you open documents in programs that they weren't created in. See page 60.

Behind the Scenes

Behind the scenes, the **System Folder** has changed a lot. It holds a bunch of new folders that neatly organize your System Folder. The Control Panel is now a folder of individual control panels, and you can open them just by double-clicking on their icons in the Control Panels folder. (Of course, you can use the Control Panel in the Apple menu, too, but it's called Control Panels now.) There are a lot of neat new control panels, too, like Views, which lets you change what you see in Finder windows. Want to change the size of Finder icons? Choose a different font for Finder windows? See folder sizes? See page 72.

Apple Menu Items is a folder that contains all the things that appear on the Apple menu. You don't have to use Font/DA Mover any more to install desk accessories. You can also put programs and documents in your Apple menu, where they're convenient. See page 26.

Startup Items is a folder in your System Folder that lets you specify which programs or documents you want to start automatically when you start your Mac. Just drag their icons there. See page 26.

System Folder

◀ **Tip:** *With System 7.5 you get a hierarchical Apple menu with Recent Documents and Recent Applications choices on it that let you look at what you used last.*

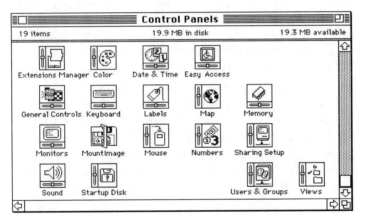

There are lots of control panels now—even more with System 7.5.

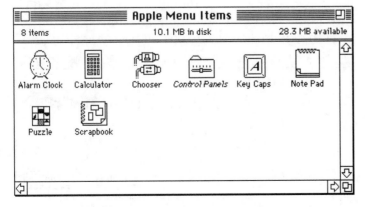

Items in the Apple menu are in a folder of their own

Tip: *In System 7.1, just drag fonts to the System Folder. They'll be put in a Fonts folder of their own.*

Another new folder in the System Folder is called Preferences; it contains preference settings that your programs put there.

An Extensions folder now holds your printer icons and file sharing utilities. See pages 26, 90.

Best of all, you can just drag icons onto the System Folder and the Mac will usually figure out which of these new folders they should go into. (Sometimes it can't guess about pre-System 7 items.)

System

And if you look closely at your System file, you'll see that it's different, too: you can open it now, and you just drag icons of sounds (and fonts, if you're still in 7.0) to put them in it. No more Font/DA Mover. See page 91.

Finding Things

Finally, the **Finder** lives up to its name! There's a new Find command (Command-F) in the File menu (and a Find Again, Command-G, along with it). You can do selective searches for all sorts of things. Want to find a file whose name ends with *Scott*? Find one that doesn't contain *Scott*? Find one that's smaller than 200K or bigger than 500K? Find version 5.0 of Word? Find a document you created on February 16 or modified on March 3, or find documents created before or after March 3? Find all the files that you've labeled "Durango Project"? Find a file that you know absolutely nothing else about except that you added comments to it that contain the word *xylophone*? You get the idea. There are all sorts of built-in criteria that you can use. And you can search for all the files on the disk that meet your criteria, not go hunting for them one at a time. Also, when Find finds something, it shows it to you, and you can double-click on it to open it *right now*. See page 47.

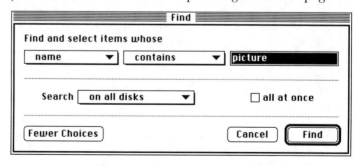

Labels

There's a new **Label menu**. What it does is let you assign a label to an item (and assign a color to it, too, if you have a color monitor). You use the Labels control panel to set up a system of labels for yourself. You might want to label your files by project code name (like Memphis, Durango, Las Vegas) or by client name (Acme Construction, Periat Plumbing) or by category (personal, business, fun). Because you can search for files by label, you can see where all the files that are related to each other are. See page 53.

◀ **Tip:** *You can view Finder windows by label, too.*

	Picture 0	5K	MacPaint 2.0 docu...	Project 1	*Labels*
	Picture 1	1K	MacPaint 2.0 docu...	Project 1	
	Picture 2	4K	MacPaint 2.0 docu...	Project 2	

Aliases

Aliases are new in System 7. What they do is let you create icons that are sort of like duplicates of a program or folder or document, but not really. They're just pointers, or links, to where the actual thing really is.

Being able to make aliases opens up all sorts of possibilities. If there's a program you use all the time, like Microsoft Word, you can put an alias of it in the Apple menu, where it's easy to get to. If there are folders you work in a lot, you can put aliases of them there, too. If you're on a network, you can set up an alias of your file server and quickly connect to it by just double-clicking on it.

Because you can have more than one alias of the same thing, you can keep duplicates of documents in different folders and reorganize your filing system so that you can keep files both by, say, date (in a November folder) and by project (in a Memphis folder, for example). Since those documents aren't copies but are pointers to the real thing, when you change one, all the others change, too, so you instantly update your document everywhere you've stored it. See page 50.

If you're on a network, you can even make an alias of your hard disk, copy it onto a floppy, take it to somebody else's computer, put the floppy in the drive, and double-click on the alias of your hard disk to connect back to your own computer. This is really incredible!

Fonts

Helvetica

System 7 introduces a new kind of font: **TrueType fonts**. They look good on the screen as well as in print. You don't have to install a screen font for your screen and a printer font for your printer any more. To install fonts (old-style or TrueType), you just drag them into your System Folder. You can keep on using your old fonts, too. See page 89.

▶ **Tip:** *Here's a cute trick: double-click on a font in your System file to see a sample of what it looks like.*

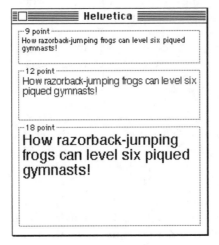

Sounds

You just drag sounds into your System Folder, too. And you can double-click on them there to hear a sample of what they sound like.

Stationery Pads

Stationery pads are new in System 7, too. They let you set up a format and use common text, like a letterhead or an invoice form. If there are standard documents you create over and over again, you can just set them up as stationery pads. To change a document you've created into a stationery pad, use the Get Info box (Command-I) and click the Stationery pad. Some programs will let you choose a Stationery option from their Save As dialog box. See page 54.

Publish and Subscribe is a new feature that some programs have. If your program has it, you'll see commands about Publishers and Subscribers in its Edit menu. If you've got this capability, you'll be able to create hot links to other documents so that when you change the information in one, the others are updated, too. Say, for example, that you're updating a spreadsheet that's also in several documents you created with your word processor. You can select the new material and publish it (it becomes a separate file with an icon of its own), and any documents that subscribe to it will be automatically updated. This is also called "live" copying and pasting. (It's called IAC, too, for Interapplication Communications. Now you know.) See page 63.

Publish and Subscribe

System 7 has so much file sharing and **networking** ability that there's a whole chapter on it in this book. You can set up "drop" folders to exchange messages with everybody else on your network. You can access your own computer from somebody else's. You can decide exactly who gets to see which of your files, or you can share what's on your whole hard disk. You can even assign secret passwords. System 7 comes with everything but the magic decoder ring. See page 113.

File Sharing

A shared folder

System 7 lets programs have the ability to link to other programs, if their designers built them that way. For example, you might have a spelling checker that will work with several different programs if you link it to them. You can use the Program Linking feature to let other computers on the network you're connected to link with your programs, and you can link to theirs, as long as the programs have this new capability. See page 124.

Program Linking

There are all sorts of utilities on your system disks. Instead of putting those System disks away as soon as you've installed System 7, check out what else is on them. See page 105.

System Tools

Tech Specs

▶ **Tip:** *System 7.5 adds support for volumes up to 4 gigabytes, a Threads Manager for concurrent application processing, 16-bit stereo quality sound, and support for telephone applications as well as PowerTalk and QuickDraw GX.*

System 7 uses what's called **virtual memory**, if your computer can handle it (if yours can't, you won't see any choices for it on the Memory control panel). What it does is let you work as if you had a great deal of memory than you really do. System 7 also lets you use **32-bit addressing**, which lets your Mac use very large amounts of RAM— much greater than 8 Mb. To find out more about these features, look in the *Special Features* booklet that came with your Mac. Not all Macs have these special memory features.

QuickTime

And don't forget QuickTime! It's an extension that lets a color Mac play "movies"—video clips or animation, or even music recordings. You can use QuickTime to cut and paste sound, video, and animation just as if you were working with text and graphics. You can get QuickTime from Apple, if you're interested in it.

In Trouble?

Sometimes even the most perfectly designed system software doesn't work right. Sometimes you don't work right, either. If you get one of those dreaded bomb icons, or if you get other unexpected results (that's a polite way of saying "if something messes up"), you may find an answer to your question in the "Oh, No! (Troubleshooting)" chapter. See page 129.

The Finder and the Desktop

The Finder is the part of your Mac's system software that manages the desktop—what you see when you first start your Macintosh. It keeps track of which file's in which folder, what disk you've put into your floppy drive, what programs you've got, and all that sort of thing. When you install System 7 or upgrade it to a later release, you get a new Finder with your new system software.

Tip: *Your system software's in a folder called the System Folder.*

You can check which version of system software your Mac's running by choosing About This Macintosh from the Apple menu. (It will also show you how much memory your system's using, and how much memory any programs you've got running are using, too. Press the Option key to see a tribute to About The Finder. (Try it and see.)

The Finder's New Look

The new System 7 Finder has all kinds of new features, tricks, and shortcuts. In fact, there are so many that it's hard to digest them all in one sitting, but here's a tip: it's sure easier to *use them* than read about them. You'll probably want to turn on your Mac as you go through this book so that you can try out some of these new things.

The most obvious new feature is the way everything looks, of course, so we'll look at that first.

You think everything still looks the same? You're viewing by icon. Try viewing by name to see where the changes are.

You still put your files in folders, just like you do in a real office (they didn't change *everything!*) But folders look a little different now, and you work with them in a new way.

Tip: *If you're new to the Mac and you don't know what the old way was, that's OK. Read on. This chapter and the next will cover the basics, both old and new.*

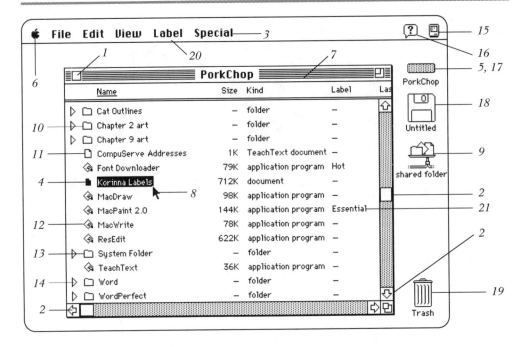

1 Click here to close a window.

2 Drag the scroll box to scroll through a window, click on the scroll arrows, or click and hold down the mouse button one of the scroll arrows. Click anywhere in the scroll bar to go to that area of what's in the window.

3 Click on a menu's name to see its choices; drag and release the mouse button to select one of them.

4 A highlighted icon means that it's selected.

5 A dimmed icon means that it's open.

6 The Apple menu has special items like desk accessories.

7 The title bar shows the name of the folder you're in. You can move a window by dragging it by its title bar.

8 The mouse pointer's controlled by the location of the mouse on your real desktop. The pointer changes to different shapes at different times.

9 Shared folder

10 Folder

11 Document

12 Program

13 Double-click here to open a folder into a new window.

14 Click here to expand the contents of the folder into the same window.

15 Click on this icon to see the Application menu, which shows you what programs are running and lets you manage windows.

16 The Finder's Help menu

17 Your hard disk (yours will have another name)

18 A floppy disk that's in your floppy disk drive

19 Drag icons to the Trash to throw them away.

20 The Label menu's new in System 7.

21 You change label text with the Views control panel.

Outline Views

A tiny triangle now appears next to each folder's name if you're looking at a **list view** (in other words, not viewing by icon or small icon), and if you click on it, you'll see what's in the folder. These are called **outline views**, because you see each level indented from the right side of the window.

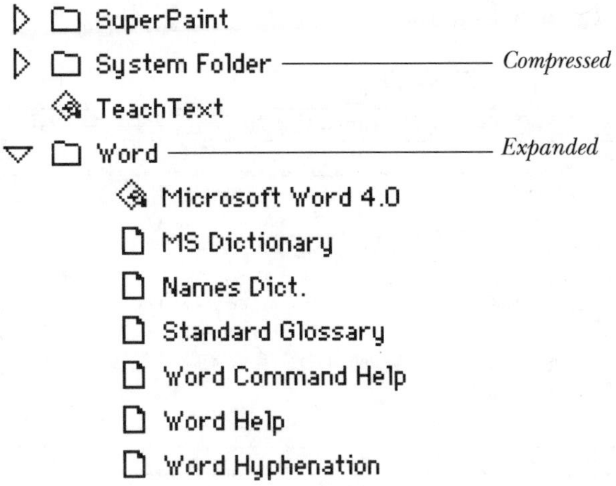

▷ ☐ SuperPaint

▷ ☐ System Folder ——————————— *Compressed*

   ⬧ TeachText

▽ ☐ Word ——————————————— *Expanded*

     ⬧ Microsoft Word 4.0

     ☐ MS Dictionary

     ☐ Names Dict.

     ☐ Standard Glossary

     ☐ Word Command Help

     ☐ Word Help

     ☐ Word Hyphenation

If there are other folders in that folder, they'll have a tiny triangle next to them, and you can look in them the same way. This is called **expanding** a folder. You won't open a new window by clicking on the triangle, so you can happily go hunting for the document or whatever you're looking for without cluttering up your screen. (Actually, you can use the new Find command to find things *even faster*: see Chapter 4.)

To go back to the original view of the folder (this is called **compressing** a folder), just click on the triangle again. It'll be pointing down if the folder is expanded. You can expand as many folders as you like without opening a new window.

If you double-click on a folder's icon or name, you'll open a new window showing what's in the folder. This is the way previous Finders worked, and you could wind up with a lot of windows open while you looked for whatever you were looking for. The System 7 way makes it easier to see the structure of your filing system without having to open all those windows.

◀ **Tip:** *Another neat trick: Hold down the Option key while you open folders. The inactive windows will magically close as you continue to hunt for the file you want.*

Seeing Where You Are

If you open a lot of windows, you can get lost in your filing system. To check where a folder is in the filing system hierarchy, just press the Command key and click on the window's title. Not in the title bar, in the title itself. A pop-up menu will appear, listing all the folders that the folder you're looking at is in. Your hard disk will be at the very bottom, if you're looking at folders on a hard disk.

▶ **Tip:** *Double-click on your hard disk icon to get back to the top level of folders quickly.*

Folder opened into new window

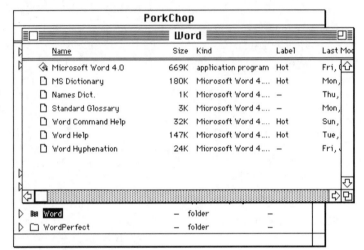

▶ **Tip:** *The active window's the one that has stripes in its title bar.*

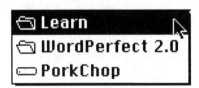

You can use this tip to move through levels of folders. Just drag through the pop-up menu to highlight the folder where you want to go and release the mouse button.

And here's another neat trick. You can *close the window you're looking at and open a new folder at the same time* if you press the Option key while you choose the new folder. This can really help keep your screen from getting cluttered, because all you'll see is the newly opened folder.

Creating a New Folder

To create a new folder, choose New Folder from the File menu, or use the keyboard shortcut Command-N, which is often a lot faster than using the mouse. The new folder will be called "untitled folder," and it'll be ready for you to type a name for it. You'll see it in the active window, too, so you don't have to go hunting after it!

(A little bit of history: Formerly, a new folder was called "Empty Folder," and it appeared wherever the E's were, which could really get confusing if you were looking under N for New Folder, which of course you would do if you were trying to be logical.)

If you make more untitled folders in the same folder, they'll be called "untitled folder 2," and so on, until you give them a name.

But magic happens when you name a new folder. Well, it's sort of magic; some folks will cry "bug!" If the name you give it begins with a letter of the alphabet that isn't being displayed on the screen, your new folder will—magically—disappear. What happens is that the Finder moves it to its proper place in the alphabet. Just type the first letter of the new name to see your new folder.

Tip: *If you want your new folder to be on the desktop, select an icon on the desktop first. Otherwise it'll show up in the active window.*

Tip: *The Save As dialog box has a New Folder button, too.*

Tip: *Lost a new folder? Type the first letter of its name.*

Deleting a Folder

For the benefit of those of you who've just bought a Mac, you delete things by dragging them to the Trash (more on trashing in Chapter 3). If you've been using one of those other kinds of computers, this may not be obvious. There's no DEL or ERASE command. Hey, there's no RENAME command, either! But don't get me started on that....

Most of the basic ways you work with windows haven't changed: you still move a window by dragging it by its title bar (press Command and drag if you don't want to make the window active as you move it) and change its size by dragging the size box. But there are a few new features.

Working with Finder Windows

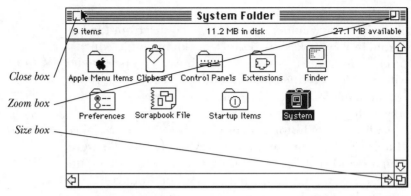

Close box

Zoom box

Size box

Zooming Windows

▶ **Tip:** *You can customize Finder windows by using the Views control panel. It lets you change fonts and pick what information you want to be displayed in list views. See the Control Panels chapter.*

Clicking on the Zoom box will enlarge a window just big enough to see what's in it. You can still see the Trash and disk icons. This is a subtle change, but if you're looking for the Trash or for another disk, you'll appreciate it.

To get a window back to its original size, just click on the Zoom box again.

Hiding Windows

Another thing you can do with System 7 is hide windows. Clicking on the tiny icon in the upper-right corner of the screen (the Application menu) will let you hide the windows of the program you're working in, or hide all the other windows except the one you're working in. This helps you keep your screen neat and tidy.

▶ **Tip:** *Hiding a program's windows keeps it in memory, so you can get at it quickly. Closing a window doesn't.*

▶ **Tip:** *In System 7.5, there's a new WindowShade feature that "rolls up" windows when you double-click in their title bars.*

To see all the windows you've opened, even the ones you've hidden, choose Show All.

Moving Windows

You can drag a window by its title bar to move it. But that also makes it the active window. To move a window without making it active, press Command and drag.

Dialog boxes that have title bars are movable now, too.

◀ **Tip:** *Drag or Command-drag a window by its title bar to move it.*

Secret Scrolling

If you can't see what you're looking for in a Finder list, try this shortcut: just select an item and drag it toward the bottom of the window. When you get to the bottom, the window will scroll. Drag something to the top to scroll it up. To scroll sideways, just click on one of the window's edges and hold the mouse button down.

If you have an extended keyboard, you can use the PgUp, PgDn, End, and Home keys to move through windows, too. You can really zip through big windows this way. Try it, even if you're a diehard mouser.

◀ **Tip:** *Another way to scroll now is to press and hold the Up or Down arrow keys down. Or, if you've got an extended keyboard, use the Home and End or PgUp and PgDn keys.*

Magic Sorting

To sort a window's contents by size, click on Size at the top of the window, if you're not viewing by icon or small icon. This will list the largest document first. If the window's showing folders, they'll be alphabetized; the Finder doesn't sort folders by size. (You can choose to see folder sizes by using the new Views control panel.)

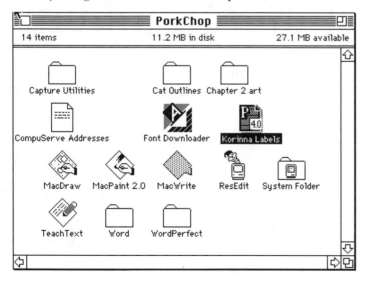

It's easy to sort icons now: Option-Clean Up. How they'll be sorted depends on what view you were looking at last, so you can sort by size, by label, or whatever.

To alphabetize a Finder window, click on Name. Magic! You can also click on Label or Kind to sort by those things. (Chapter 4 has some more hints on how you can use the new Label menu.)

If you're viewing by icon, here's how to alphabetize your icons: first, view by name; then view by icon, press the Option key, and choose Clean Up by Name from the Special menu.

Closing Windows

▶ **Tip:** *To close all the open windows, press Option and click the active window's Close box. Pressing Option-Command-W does the same thing.*

Closing windows works pretty much the same as it always did. To close a window, click in its Close box (in the up-per-left corner) or press Command-W. Option-Command-W will close *all* the windows you've got open.

Closing a window isn't the same thing as hiding one. When a program's hidden, it's still in memory, ready to use. If you make it active again, its windows reappear.

Inactive Windows

▶ **Tip:** *When you click on an item in a window that's not active, it doesn't become active until you release the mouse button. Makes it easier to drag items out of inactive windows, doesn't it?*

With System 7, when you click on an item in a window that's not active, the window won't become active unless you release the mouse button while the pointer's still in the window. This makes it a lot easier to drag items out of inactive windows. Before, when you clicked on an item in a window, that window would become the active window and would automatically jump to the top of the pile of win-dows on your desktop. So you either had to carefully arrange windows so that you could see the window where you wanted to drag the icon, or you had to drag icons out to the desktop and then drag them back into the windows where you wanted them to go. You can still do both of these, but the new way's a lot easier!

Selecting

▶ **Tip:** *You can do this in the Chooser, too, and in Open and Save dialog boxes.*

There are all kinds of new ways to select things, too. You can just type a letter to select the first item in a list that be-gins with that letter. This can really help if you're looking at the contents of your hard disk up near the A's and want to choose the Word folder. To move to another letter of the alphabet, just type that letter, or press Tab to move to the next item in alphabetical order. How is this different? Say you're in the R's and you want to move to another item beginning with R. If you type R again, nothing happens. Press Tab instead. Shift-Tab will move you backward.

Dragging to Select

To select a bunch of icons that are right next to each other, just click outside one of them and drag over them. You'll see a selection box around them. You can scroll a window this way, too. Just drag to the border in the direction you want to go. In a list view, you have to select the icon itself to do this.

Selecting in Different Folders

The new outline views now let you select several items that are in different folders. The trick is to open all the folders you want to select from in one window (use those triangles. Just open the folders and Shift-click to select multiple items. This is really handy for doing big cleanup jobs, because you only have to drag one big selection to the Trash. It's good for mass moves, too.

Tip: With System 7.5, you can copy by dragging a selection to the desktop, where it becomes a clipping, or you can drag it to another application that supports this new drag-and-drop feature.

Tip: You can drag to select in list views now.

Tip: Drag to move; Option-drag to copy on the same disk.

PorkChop			
Name	Size	Kind	Label
◈ MacPaint 2.0	144K	application program	Essent
✿ MacWrite	78K	application program	–
◈ ResEdit	622K	application program	–
▷ ☐ System Folder	–	folder	–
◈ TeachText	36K	application program	–
▽ ☐ Word	–	folder	–
◈ Microsoft Word 4.0	669K	application program	Hot
☐ MS Dictionary	180K	Microsoft Word 4....	Hot
☐ Names Dict.	1K	Microsoft Word 4....	–
☐ Standard Glossary	3K	Microsoft Word 4....	–
☐ Word Command Help	32K	Microsoft Word 4....	Hot
☐ Word Help	147K	Microsoft Word 4....	Hot
☐ Word Hyphenation	24K	Microsoft Word 4....	–
▷ ☐ WordPerfect	–	folder	–

You can select items in different folders by Shift-clicking in outline views.

Selecting Everything

The Edit menu's got a Select All command that will select everything in a window. It's been around a while, but I'm surprised at how many people don't use it. It saves a lot of time if you're copying or moving a lot of items that are all in the same window. You can just go back and deselect the few that you don't want.

Here's another good tip for using Select All. You shouldn't have more than one System Folder per disk, or you'll confuse your Mac. Well, some programs that you buy come on disks that have a System Folder on them, so that you can use that disk as a startup disk. You don't need or want to copy that folder onto your hard disk, but you do want to copy everything else that's on the disk. Just insert the disk, double-click on its icon, press Command-A to select all, and then Shift-click on the System Folder icon to deselect it. You can then drag everything else off the disk and into a folder on your hard disk.

▶ **Tip:** *Keyboard shortcut: Command-A.*

Dialog Box Tricks

As you work with your Mac, you'll often see dialog boxes asking you for more information or giving you a list of things to choose from. They have different kinds of buttons that let you choose different things.

If a button has a heavy border around it, you can just press Return to choose it.

Radio buttons let you choose one of several options.

LaserWriter Page Setup   7.0   OK

Paper: ● US Letter ○ A4 Letter ○ | Tabloid ▼ | Cancel
      ○ US Legal ○ B5 Letter

Reduce or [100] %   Printer Effects: Options
Enlarge: ⊠ Font Substitution?

Orientation   ⊠ Text Smoothing?
   ⊠ Graphics Smoothing?
   ⊠ Faster Bitmap Printing?

Check boxes let you click to turn them on and off.

A downward-pointing arrow indicates more choices if you click here.

Here are a few tricks for working with dialog boxes. Some of these tips are new; some of them are old; but some of them may be new to some of you.

Movable Dialog Boxes

You can move a dialog box if it has a title bar. Just drag it by the title bar like any other window. If there's a zoom box on it, you can resize it, too.

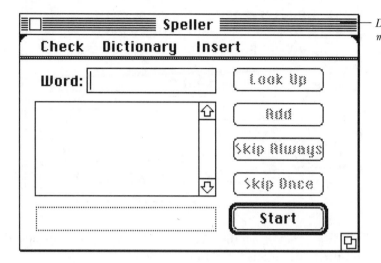

Drag the title bar to move a movable dialog box

Pop-Up Menus

A shadowed border around a text item means that a pop-up menu will appear to choose from if you click on the item. Pop-up menus work like radio buttons: you can usually choose only one option on the menu.

Quick Selecting

You can type the first letter of a file's name to select it quickly in an Open dialog box, just like in a Finder window.

◀ **Tip:** *Try this typing trick; it'll save you lots of time. You may never go back to scrolling again.*

Moving through the Filing System

You can move up through the hierarchical filing system by clicking on the tiny disk icon in a System 7 Open or Save As dialog box (also called a directory dialog box).

You can also click on the icon next to the folder's name at the top of the dialog box. This brings up a pop-up menu showing all the folders that contain the folder you're in.

Click here to see where you are in your filing system

...or click here instead.

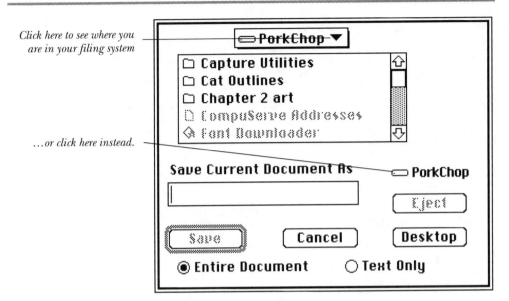

To go back *down* the hierarchical system, double-click on the folder icons listed in the dialog box.

Doing Nothing

If you don't want to do anything in a dialog box, you can click Cancel. But pressing Command-period will do the same thing, and it's faster than reaching for the mouse if you're typing. This can also sometimes get you out of a dialog box that isn't giving you any choices about what to do next, like the ones you get when the Mac insists on swapping disks until the cows come home.

Finder Keyboard Shortcuts

▶ **Tip:** *To see even more Finder keyboard shortcuts, choose Finder Shortcuts from the Help menu. You'll get several screens of them.*

A lot of folks get so used to the mouse that they forget there are plenty of things they can do without taking their hands off the keyboard. Here are a few new Finder tricks. All of these tricks are easier to understand (and remember) if you try them out than if you just read about them.

Instead of scrolling with the mouse by dragging the scroll box or using the scroll arrows, you can just press the arrow keys to move to the next icon in the arrow's direction. In fact, you can scroll through a window this way.

Pressing Command-Down arrow will open a folder

that's selected, displaying its contents in a new window. This is the same as double-clicking with the mouse.

Pressing Command-Up arrow moves you one level up, so if you're looking at a window of what's in a folder and you want to go back to the window that the folder was in, this is a neat keyboard shortcut.

Command-Option-Right arrow opens up all of a selected folder's folders, and Command-Option-Left arrow collapses a folder and all the folders in it.

And here are some handy new shortcuts that will keep the screen clean, too: Use Command-Option-Up arrow to close a folder or disk and close the current window at the same time. And pressing Command-Option-Down arrow will open a folder or disk and close the current window. This cleans up your screen in a hurry, without a lot of mouse clicks.

Tip: *To move up one level of folders, you can press Command-Up arrow.*

Tip: *To get back to the desktop in a hurry if you're deep within your folders, there's a new shortcut: press Command-Shift-Up arrow. Try it and see.*

Initializing and Erasing Disks

The Finder also's in charge of preparing disks for use with your Mac. When you insert a new, blank disk, you'll be told that it's unreadable and asked if you want to initialize it. Click One-Sided or Two-Sided if you do, or Eject (or just press Return) if you don't. **Initializing a disk wipes out whatever's already on it.**

Tip: *With System 7.5, you get PC Exchange, which lets you format and open DOS disks on your Mac.*

This disk is unreadable:
Do you want to initialize it?

Eject   One-Sided   Two-Sided

Most disks nowadays are two-sided (800K). The older single-sided disks hold only 400K of data. High-density disks hold 1.4 Mb, and you can use these only if you've got an Apple SuperDrive or another disk drive that accepts high-density disks. How can you tell which is which? High-density disks usually have HD somewhere on them, and they also have *two* square holes.

Sometimes you'll get that "unreadable" message if a disk is bad. If there's something on it you want to save,

Warning: *Don't initialize 1.4 Mb disks as 800K (two-sided) disks.*

don't initialize it! Instead, try this sneaky trick. Start the program that originally created the document you need that's on the bad disk and then choose Open from that program's File menu and try to open the document. If this works, save the documents you want to recover onto a different disk. Throw the bad disk away so you don't use it again!

Erasing vs. Trashing a Disk

Choosing Erase Disk from the Special menu reinitializes a disk, and everything on it's wiped out. Dragging a disk's contents to the Trash just puts them in the Trash, and you can get them back later, even if the lights go out. Really. System 7's Trash Collector doesn't empty the Trash until you choose Empty Trash from the Special menu. And it saves the Trash whenever you turn off your computer.

Locking Disks

Sometimes you may get messages about a disk's being locked. The Finder won't let you save any changes to the files on it, or it won't let you trash a file that's on it. To unlock a disk, close the little slot at the top of the disk. To lock one, close the slot.

It's a good idea to keep disks that contain your programs and system software locked so that the files on them don't get changed. Lock them before you ever put them in a disk drive.

Your Startup Disk

Finder   System

For a disk to be a startup disk, able to start your Mac, it has to contain two things: a System file icon and a Finder icon in the same folder. Usually this folder's called the System Folder, but the Mac will recognize any folder that has a Finder and a System file in it as the system folder, even if you've named it something else.

When your computer starts up, it reads what's in the System Folder, including any system extensions (INITs and CDEVs) that extend the system's capabilities and uses that information to set itself up.

Usually your Mac starts up from your hard disk, but you can start with a floppy disk, if it's in the drive when you turn your Mac on.

Your startup disk is represented by the icon in the far upper-right corner of the screen.

In addition to the Finder, a System 7 System Folder contains a lot of other things, and it's organized into a structure of folders, unlike earlier System Folders.

(By the way, this is the way Apple capitalizes it: System Folder for that very important one; lowercase "folder" for all the others.)

Your System Folder

System Folder

◀ Tip: *You can just drag an item (other than a document or a program) onto the System Folder's icon, and it'll automatically be placed in the folder it belongs in. But don't drag it to the System Folder's open window; drag it to its icon.*

You can choose which items you want to have in these folders in your System Folder. For example, you might want to delete some desk accessories that you never use on the Apple menu, like Puzzle, or remove a control panel like Easy Access, which lets you do one-handed typing.

◀ Tip: *With System 7.5, you can lock your System Folder to keep it from being changed. Use the new General Controls panel.*

The Control Panels Folder

Control panels, which let you customize how your Mac works, are all in a new Control Panels folder. Chapter 6 is on the new System 7.1 control panels. Even more new or improved control panels come with System 7.5; see Chapter 11 for those.

Control Panels

Apple Menu Items

The Apple Menu Items Folder

Items that are on the Apple menu, like the Calculator and Alarm Clock, are in the Apple Menu Items folder. You can add more items to your Apple menu, including desk accessories, documents, folders, and programs. Just drag their icons (or aliases of them; see Chapter 4) into the Apple Menu Items folder. You don't even have to restart your Mac. To take an item off the Apple menu, drag its icon out of the folder.

▶ **Tip:** *You can open a desk accessory just by clicking on its icon.*

By the way, you don't have to use Font/DA mover to install the desk accessories that you see on the Apple menu any more. Just drag their icons into your Apple Menu Items folder.

▶ **Tip:** *In System 7.1, you can just drag font suitcases to the System Folder and drop them..*

If you want to use a desk accessory from an earlier version of system software, find the suitcase file that holds it and open it. Then just drag the icon of the DA you want to use out. You can put DA icons on the desktop or in the System Folder, where they'll be relocated into the Apple Menu Items folder.

Alison Font

The Startup Items Folder

Want to start a program or open a document when you start up your Mac? Just drag the item (or an alias of it) into the Startup Items folder in the System Folder.

Startup Items

To stop something from being opened on startup, drag its icon out of the Startup Items folder. Be sure to take it completely out of the System Folder so that the Mac doesn't find it and helpfully put it back in the folder it belongs in.

The Extensions Folder

Utilities that let you share files with other users on a network and programs called printer drivers that control different kinds of printers, are in a folder called Extensions. Here's where PrintMonitor is stored (if you're using a LaserWriter) and also Finder Help (those balloons).

Extensions

The Preferences Folder

Files that programs create to control how they and your Macintosh work together (you can't open these), are in a Preferences folder.

Preferences

The Clipboard and Scrapbook

The Clipboard, which is where each thing you copy or cut goes (one at a time) so that you can paste it somewhere else, and the Scrapbook, which lets you save items that are cut or copied, are "loose" in the System Folder, just like always.

Clipboard

You can see what's on the Clipboard by choosing Show Clipboard from the Edit menu. To look in the Scrapbook, use the Apple menu, or double-click on its icon in the Apple Menu Items folder.

Scrapbook File

The Scrapbook holds only a few items at a time, but you can get around that. Just take it out of the Apple Menu Items folder and rename it something else when it's full. Name the file that you want to use as the Scrapbook "Scrapbook File" (don't use quotes) and put it in the Apple Menu Items folder.

◀ **Tip:** *In System 7.5, the Scrapbook's been improved. You can copy from it by dragging and dropping.*

	Name	Size	Kind	Label	Last Modified
□	Chicago	44K	font	–	–
□	Courier	58K	font	–	–
□	Courier 9	5K	font	–	–
□	Courier (bold)	56K	font	–	–
□	Courier 10	5K	font	–	–
□	Courier 12	6K	font	–	–
□	Courier 14	6K	font	–	–
□	Courier 18	7K	font	–	–
□	Courier 24	10K	font	–	–
□	Geneva	54K	font	–	–
□	Geneva (italic) 9	3K	font	–	–
□	Geneva 10	3K	font	–	–
□	Geneva 14	4K	font	–	–
□	Geneva 18	5K	font	–	–

System

◀ **Tip:** *You can click on a font to see how it looks, or click on a sound to hear it.*

The System File

The System file, which now contains fonts and sounds, is also loose in the System Folder. You can open it by double-clicking on it. You can just drag fonts and sounds to the System Folder, and the Mac will put them where they belong. In System 7.0, they go into the System file; in 7.1 and 7.5, fonts go into a separate Fonts folder.

◀ **Tip:** *After System 7.1, the System file holds only the basic (system) fonts, and the rest are in a separate Fonts folder inside the System Folder.*

Starting Up

If you've been using a Mac for a while, you probably already know that there are a couple of different ways to start your Mac and make it jump through hoops. Here they are, as the ad says, again for the first time.

Closing Open Windows

Usually your Mac will open the same windows that you had open when you shut down last, and if you had a lot of them open, starting up can be slow. To avoid opening all those windows on startup, just hold down the Option key while you start up.

Rebuilding the Desktop

▶ **Tip:** *See the Oh, No! (Troubleshooting) chapter for other tips on when you may need to rebuild the desktop.*

You can rebuild your desktop by holding down the Command and Option keys while your Mac is starting. Rebuilding your desktop helps your system keep track of where everything is. It's a good thing to do once in a while, even though your desktop file is a little different with System 7. Also, if you get a system error message with a bomb when you insert a disk, try rebuilding the desktop.

Turning off System Extensions

▶ **Tip:** *System 7.1 comes with an Extensions Manager control panel that lets you turn extensions on and off selectively. An improved one comes with System 7.5.*

If you want to turn off all your system extensions (also called INITs and cdevs) hold down the Shift key while you start your Macintosh. Some of these interfere with your System Folder and can cause strange things to happen, like your computer freezing up when you try to copy a disk. If you're getting odd results or bombs, try starting this way. If everything works fine, you'll know it's something you added that's causing the trouble (see the Troubleshooting chapter for how to figure out which one it is.)

Switching Startup Disks

▶ **Tip:** *You can't choose between using the Finder and MultiFinder any more in System 7. Multitasking's built in now.*

If you've got two hard disks, you can switch to using the other as a startup disk (fire up what's in its System Folder) by using the Startup Disk control panel and restart your computer. You can just start a program that's on the other hard disk while you hold down the Option key, and it will switch to the other disk's System Folder, too.

Why would you want to do this? Since you can put different things in your System Folder (like different desk accessories and items in the Apple menu), you can have startup disks that are configured in different ways, depending on how you want to work when one's in control.

Also, changing basic things in the system software on the disk that's running the system while it's running it is sort of like doing an appendectomy on yourself while you're still conscious. But it's OK to change things like control panels in the active System Folder. In fact, a lot of these control panels now make your changes immediately, without your having to restart your computer for changes to take effect.

Starting from a Floppy Disk

Instead of starting your Mac from your hard disk, you can start it from a floppy disk that has a System file and a Finder on it, preferably in a folder named System Folder. If you're having problems with your hard disk, this may be the only way you can start. Just turn your Mac off, put the floppy disk in the drive, and then power up your Mac again. It will start from that disk instead of from your hard disk. If you forget to put the disk in the drive before you turn your Mac on, you can quickly shove it in as your computer's starting, if your timing's right and you get it in before the startup sequence begins (right after the beep). If your hard disk icon is the one at the upper right of the screen, you weren't quick enough, and your computer started from your hard disk again. Choose Restart and shove the floppy disk back in when the Mac spits it out.

Tip: System 7's too big to fit on a regular floppy disk. Use a copy of your Disk Tools disk as a startup floppy.

Starting with a Program

If there are programs and documents that you always want to be open each time you start your Mac, just drag their icons into the new Startup Items folder inside the System Folder.

Startup Items

You can put desk accessories in there, too. And aliases, so you don't have to move items away from where they're normally stored.

Restarting   What's the difference between restarting and shutting down? Well, restarting is easier on your hard disk because it doesn't really turn it off. Shutting down is what you do when you're going to be away for a few hours. If you've adjusted a control panel that tells you to restart your Mac for the changes to take effect, use the Restart command on the Special menu; don't shut down.

Shutting Down   It's rude to your system software to shut down without using the Shut Down command on the Special menu. And besides, you could lose some work and damage files that way. So don't shut down without it. System 7 will helpfully exit your programs, close all your open windows and tidy everything up, and then, depending on which model of Macintosh you have, it will either shut itself off or give you a new (and this time, grammatical) message that it's safe to turn off your computer.

		Finder Techniques and Shortcuts
Create a new folder	Choose New Folder from the File menu, or press Command-N	
See what's in a folder in an outline view (expand it)	Click on the tiny triangle next to the folder icon	
Close a folder in an outline view (compress it)	Click on the tiny triangle next to the folder icon	
Open a selected icon	Double-click or Command-Down arrow	
Open a folder into a new window	Double-click on it, or press Command-Down arrow when it's highlighted	
Close inactive windows when you open a new folder	Option-double-click on the new folder	
Get back to the desktop from a folder in a hurry	Press Command-Shift-Up arrow	
See where you are in your filing system	Command-click on the window title	
Expand or collapse a selected folder	Command-Right arrow or Command-Left arrow, or click on the triangle	
Expand or collapse the folder and all the folders in it	Command-Option-Right arrow or Command-Option-Left arrow	
Enlarge a window	Click on its Zoom box or drag it outward by a corner	
Move a window	Drag it by its title bar	
Move a window without making it active	Press Command and drag it by its title bar	
Scroll without using the scroll bars	Drag a list item to the edge of a window	

Sort a Finder window	Click on Name, Size, etc., at the top of the window. To sort an icon view, press Option and choose Clean Up
Close the active window	Click in its Close box, or press Command-W
Hide a program's windows	Choose Hide from the pop-up menu that appears when you click on the icon in the upper-right of the screen
Close all the open windows	Option-click in the active window's Close box
See all open windows, including hidden ones	Choose Show All from the pop-up menu that appears when you select the icon in the upper-right corner of the screen
Move up to the next level in your filing system	Command-Up arrow or, in an Open or Save dialog box click on the disk icon, or click on the directory name icon
Select items next to each other	Drag over them or Shift-click
Select items from different folders	Use the outline view and Shift-click
Go directly to a letter of the alphabet in a list	Type the letter, or type the first few letters of the word
Go to the next item alphabetically	Press Tab or Down arrow
Select everything in a window	Press Command-A, or choose Select All from the Edit menu
Go to the last file in a list	Press Tilde (~) or End

Move from one area to another in a dialog box	Tab or Shift-Tab (to move backward)
Get out of a dialog box without doing anything	Press Command-period or click Cancel
Choose a thick-bordered item in a dialog box	Press Return or Enter, or click on the item
Start without opening the windows you had open before	Hold down the Option key as you start up
Rebuild your desktop as you start your Mac	Press the Command and Option keys while it starts up
Turn off any system extensions (INITs)	Press the Shift key while your Mac starts up, or use the Extensions Manager
Switch startup disks	Use the Startup Disk control panel
Start from a floppy disk	Put it in the drive and turn on your Mac
Start programs and documents automatically	Put their icons (or aliases) in the Startup Items folder in your System Folder

Icons

Icons are basic to just about everything you do with your Mac. Sure enough, System 7 changed just a little about them. Actually, it changed a lot about them, but it politely did that behind the scenes, so you don't have to worry about it. One thing it did that you'll like was *let you create your own icons.*

Just in case you're joining us as a relatively new Mac user, this chapter's for you. It will quickly review icon basics and show you a few tricks with them before we get to the creating-your-own stuff. (If you're already familiar with the Mac and you can't wait, it's at the end of this chapter.)

Icon Basics

An icon is a graphic representation of a program, a document, a printer, a control panel, a disk—anything you work with. Instead of having to type a command like you have to do on a lot of Other Computers, you can just click on icons to do your work.

Selecting Icons

When an icon's selected it's highlighted (or in color). When an icon's open, it's grayed or dimmed.

PorkChop

Opened

PorkChop

Selected

Before you can work with an icon, you have to select it. After that, you can drag it, copy it, use commands from the menus on it, and so forth.

◀ **Tip:** *The icon of a disk that you insert is automatically selected.*

Clicking and Shift-Clicking

To select an icon, just click on it once. To select several icons, Shift-click on them.

And here's something new: to select several icons that are in different folders, Shift-click on them, too! If you're an old Mac hand, you probably remember that you couldn't do this before. The trick is to use the outline view so that all your icons are in the same window. Then Shift-click away.

Dragging

You can drag to select icons that are next to each other. Just put the mouse pointer at one corner of a group of icons and drag to the opposite corner. You'll see a framing rectangle when you start to drag. Once the icons are highlighted, you can drag them to other places on the desktop, like in other folders or to the Trash.

▶ **Tip:** *You can drag a dimmed icon just like any other icon.*

Copying Icons

To copy an icon, select it and then choose Duplicate from the File menu. Command-D is the keyboard shortcut. You'll get a copy of the icon named "copy" of whatever you duplicated, ready to be renamed.

▶ **Tip:** *Use the Duplicate command (Command-D) on the File menu, not Copy on the Edit menu.*

If you want to put the copy in another folder at the same time, drag the icon to the other folder while holding down the Option key. Otherwise the Mac thinks you want to move the icon to another folder, and it happily removes it from where it was and puts it in the new folder.

With System 7, you can do **background copying**: while you're running a program, you can go out to the Finder, start a copy operation, and switch back to your program. The Finder will happily keep on copying whatever you told it to while you work on something else.

◀ **Tip:** *The trick is to be in your program before you start copying. Once the Finder starts copying, it won't let you start a new program.*

Moving Icons

Perhaps it's obvious, but to move an icon, you just drag it to where you want it to go.

If you've dragged an icon out onto the desktop, you can put it back into the folder it came from by selecting it and then choosing Put Away (Command-Y is its keyboard shortcut). This is a great thing to know if you've forgotten exactly which folder the darn thing was in to begin with.

If you're dragging icons into a window that's not displaying icons (a window that's being viewed by name, for example), drag them just beneath the title bar and then release the mouse button. Otherwise it's easy to lose them in the other folders that are already in that window. If you select a folder by chance while you're dragging, they'll get put in that folder. (But if you lose them, the Find command will be glad to find them for you. See Chapter 4.)

Renaming Icons

To rename an icon—a file, a folder, a disk, your hard disk, whatever—just click on its name and then type the new name, or drag to highlight just the part you want to change and type that part. With System 7, the text of the name is put in a box, so that you know you're changing the name when you type.

◀ **Tip:** *Don't use a period (.) as the first character of a file or folder's name.*

If you make a mistake, just backspace over it and retype it. When you press Return or click somewhere with the mouse, the thing's renamed.

If you rename something by mistake—say you select something and then press a key like ? or the cat steps on the keyboard, just press Command-Z for Undo to get the

▶ **Tip:** *You can select an icon and press Return to get that box around it, too. So to quickly rename something, type its name (that takes you right to it), press Return, type the new name, and press Return again. Magic.*

original name back. As long as you haven't done anything else, this works fine.

You can use all the characters on the keyboard except the colon (:) in a name. If you type a colon, the Mac converts it to a hyphen.

System 7 will let you start a name with a space, so if you want a name to appear at the top of a list, type a space before its name. You can also get things to appear at tops of lists by starting their names with an exclamation mark (!) or a pound sign (#) or another non-letter character.

Locking an Icon

▶ **Tip:** *Shortcut: Command-I*

If you want to fix things so an icon's name can't be changed, lock it. Select the icon and then choose Get Info (Command-I is the shortcut). Click in the Locked box.

```
┌──────────────────────────────────────────┐
│ ▦□▦▦  Korinna Labels Info  ▦▦▦            │
├──────────────────────────────────────────┤
│   ┌──┐                                    │
│   │P │   Korinna Labels                   │
│   │4.0│                                   │
│   └──┘                                    │
│       Kind : document                     │
│       Size : 712K on disk (728,576 bytes used) │
│                                           │
│      Where : PorkChop :                   │
│                                           │
│    Created : Sun, Oct 14, 1990, 12:52 PM  │
│   Modified : Sun, Oct 14, 1990, 1:16 PM   │
│    Version : n/a                          │
│                                           │
│   Comments :                              │
│   ┌────────────────────────────────────┐  │
│   │                                    │  │
│   │                                    │  │
│   │                                    │  │
│   └────────────────────────────────────┘  │
│   ☐ Locked            ☐ Stationery pad    │
└──────────────────────────────────────────┘
```

▶ **Tip:** *You can click on Stationery pad to make the document into a template.*

▶ **Tip:** *When a file is locked, you can't save it (but you can use the Save As command and save it under a different name) and you can't Trash it, either.*

After you close the Get Info window, you won't be able to change the name. If you try to open the icon, you'll get a message complaining that you can't save the thing because it's locked, so why bother opening it, but if you really want to, you can. (You may have been making templates this way before.)

To unlock it, uncheck that Locked box.

You can lock programs, too, by using the Get Info window, but it's better not to. If you lock a program, you may affect how it operates. All locking a program does is stop it from being thrown away, and you're better off locking the floppy disk it came on. (To lock a disk, open the square write-protect hole.)

You can't lock a folder, but you can lock all the items in it, and you can restrict access to folders if you're on a network. See the Netiquette chapter.

Comments

The Get Info window also lets you write comments about a document. Just type them in the Comments box. Because the Find command will search through comments, this can help you identify a document quickly.

◀ **Tip:** *You can also use the Get Info window to turn a document into a stationery pad. See Chapter 4.*

Opening an Icon

With System 7, you can usually open a document and start a program at the same time by dragging the document's icon onto the program's icon and "dropping" it.

To open a bunch of folders at once, select them all and then double-click on *one* of them. Neat, huh?

◀ **Tip:** *To open an icon so that you can work with what it represents, double-click on it, or press Command-Down arrow when it's highlighted.*

If you don't like where an icon is in a window, you can just drag it to move it. Sometimes icons get spaced so closely together that you can't read their names, especially if you've used long names.

Arranging Icons

Clean Up

Another thing you can do is have the Mac align all your icons for you. To do this, use the Clean Up Window command in the Special menu. (You have to be viewing a window by icon or by small icon to get this choice. If you're on the desktop, you'll get another choice: Clean Up Desktop.)

If you want to align all the icons on an invisible grid, all next to each other, hold down the Option key while you choose Clean Up. If you just use Clean Up Window, the icons move to the nearest space on that grid, and sometimes you get blank spaces where icons could fit.

If you *don't* want an icon to snap to the invisible grid (and you've got that option turned on), hold down the Command key while you drag the icon.

◀ **Tip:** *To customize how you want icons to be displayed—whether they're staggered or in neat rows and columns, use the Views control panel.*

◀ **Tip:** *Option-Clean Up Window gets you neat rows and columns.*

To clean up just the icons you've selected, press Shift while you choose Clean Up.

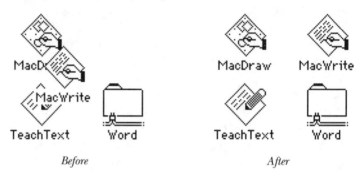

Before   *After*

Icons on the Desktop

To clean up the desktop, hold down the Option key and choose Clean Up Desktop to line up all the icons on the right side of the screen.

You can drag an icon out to the desktop so that you can find it quickly. Desktop icons have a quirk that you may overlook, though: If you copy a folder onto another disk, any icons that belong in that folder but are out on the desktop won't get copied. Be vigilant.

If you find that you're often hunting for a certain icon, make an alias for it and keep it on the desktop. This is a new System 7 feature that's explained in more detail in Chapter 4.

To return an icon on the desktop to the folder it came from, select it and then choose Put Away from the File menu (or press Command-Y).

The Trash Icon

The Trash is a special icon that lets you delete things. To delete an icon, just drag it to the Trash icon at the bottom of your screen. With System 7, the Trash isn't emptied until you choose Empty Trash from the Special menu (even if you shut down your computer), so you can get back things you put in the Trash if you change your mind.

To open the Trash and see what's in there, just double-click on its icon.

When you empty the Trash, you'll get a dialog box asking you if you're sure you want to do that and telling you how many items are in there. If you don't want to get this warning, hold down the Option key when you choose Empty Trash.

◀ **Tip:** *You can move the Trash to a different location on your desktop.*

```
▤☐▨▨▨▨ Trash Info ▨▨▨▨▨
   ╔═══╗
   ║(()║   Trash
   ╚═══╝
  Where: On the desktop

  Contents: 1 file and 0 folders are in the Trash
            for a total of 2K.



  Modified: Fri, Apr 19, 1991, 8:55 AM

  ☒ Warn before emptying
```

You can suppress the warnings by selecting the Trash icon and choosing Get Info (Command-I). Click in the "Warn before emptying" box to remove the X, and you won't get asked about it any more.

Disk Icons

You can manipulate the icons that represent disks, but there are a few subtle differences between them and other icons. First, when you insert a disk, it's automatically selected, because the Mac thinks you're going to want to do something with it right away. Also, if you eject a disk from your disk drive by choosing Eject Disk from the Special menu (Command-E is its shortcut; Shift-Command-1 will do it, too), you'll see that its icon stays dimmed on your desktop. The Mac will remember what's on that disk as long as the icon is there. It may ask you to reinsert the disk if it needs to read it for something else.

If you know you're not going to be using anything that's on a disk, eject it this way: drag it to the Trash. Its icon will disappear from your desktop (and from the Mac's memory, too). Otherwise you may get pesky messages about reinserting that disk. (To turn off these messages, try pressing Command-period. You may have to do it more than once.)

◀ **Tip:** *For the quickest disk eject, drag the disk's icon to the Trash or press Command-Y.*

Another trick way to eject a disk is to select its icon and choose Put Away, or Command-Y. And you can also eject a disk from an Open or Save As dialog box within a program; there's an Eject button if you've selected a floppy disk. Ejecting a disk this way is the same as choosing Eject Disk from the Special menu; the disk icon is dimmed, and it stays in memory.

> **Tip:** *The icon of the startup disk is the one that's in the upper-right corner, at the very top.*

There's one icon you can't drag to the Trash: the icon of your startup disk. If you try it, you'll get a message telling you the Mac really needs that one.

To copy a floppy disk, you just drag the icon of the one you're copying over the icon of the one that you want to be the copy. There's just one thing to keep in mind: what's on the disk that's going to be the copy will be *completely replaced*, not added to. You don't have to erase it first.

> **Tip:** *To copy a disk, drag the icon of the disk you want to copy over the icon of the disk that you want to be the copy. Better yet, get Apple Disk Copy! It's a utility program that copies entire disks quickly.*

If you have only one floppy disk drive, here's how to copy disks with the least amount of swapping. Put the disk that's going to be the copy in the drive and then, when you see its icon, eject the disk with Command-E. Then insert the disk that has the stuff you want to copy and drag its icon over the dimmed icon of the disk you ejected.

Special Icons

Sometimes, when you start your Mac, you'll see a different icon instead of the usual startup screen and the "happy Mac" icon. If you see a disk with a question mark on it, the computer is waiting for you to insert a startup disk.

A disk icon with an X on it means that it isn't a startup disk, or that it's damaged. Try starting with a different startup disk.

> **Tip:** *See the Oh, No! chapter for a few more things that can go wrong and how to fix them.*

A "sad Mac" icon means that there's some problem with your system software. Better get some help. Sometimes you'll need to eject the disk that's in the drive because everything is stuck. Turn off your Mac and then turn it back on again. If the disk doesn't eject, try this. Get out your "Macintosh friend" (a sturdy paper clip), straighten one end of it, and insert it in the little tiny hole on the right of your floppy disk drive. Push gently. That's how to eject a disk manually.

Color Icons

If you have a color monitor, you can assign a color to an icon. Just select the icon and choose a color from the Label menu. To change the colors on the Label menu, use the Views control panel (see the Control Panels chapter).

◀ **Tip:** *Color your icons to group them together.*

If you use color labels, you can choose by Label from the View menu to sort them by color. They'll be sorted in the same order as the colors on the Label menu. This is a handy way to group related icons together when you're using a list view. (A list view is anything except a by icon or by small icon view).

Creating Your Own Icons

OK, here it is. You can create your own icons in System 7. Just use a graphics program like MacPaint, create the icon, and copy it (it'll be put on the Clipboard). Choose the icon you want to replace, choose Get Info (Command-I), click the icon in the Get Info window, and paste your new icon in with Command-V.

◀ **Tip:** *If your graphics program can do color, you can have color in your icons.*

To change an icon back to the original, select it in the Get Info window and choose Cut (Command-X).

It's also simple to create new icons and color them with ResEdit, the Macintosh resource editor. ResEdit will even let you change icons that represent programs, which you can't do with the Get Info window. If you're really interested in customizing your Mac, you may want to explore using ResEdit. It's available from Apple Computer or from large user groups such as the Boston Computer Society/Mac at (617) 625-7080 or BMUG (Berkeley Macintosh Users Group) at (415) 549-2684.

◀ **Tip:** *If you want to be able to read text on your new icon, use a large point size like 18 or 24 points.*

Techniques and Shortcuts

Select several icons next to each other	Drag over them or Shift-click
Select icons in different folders	Shift-click while looking at an outline view
Copy an icon in the same folder	Choose Duplicate (Command-D) from the File menu
Copy an icon into another folder	Option-drag it (on same disk)
Move an icon	Drag it
Put an icon back where it came from	Choose Put Away from the Special menu (Command-Y)
Rename an icon	Click on its name and type a new name
Undo an icon's name just after you've typed it	Choose Undo from the Edit menu (Command-Z)
Lock an icon	Select it, press Command-I, and click the Locked box
Open an icon	Double-click on it or press Command-Down arrow
Open several folders at once	Select them all and double-click on one of them
Alphabetize your icons	View by Name; then press Option and choose Clean Up by Name from the Special menu
Customize your icon views	Use the Views control panel
Clean up selected icons	Select them, press Shift, and choose Clean Up from the Special menu
Snap icons to an invisible grid and sort them	Press Option and choose Clean Up
Keep an icon from snapping to the invisible grid	Press Command while you drag it

Delete an icon	Drag it to the Trash
Empty the Trash	Choose Empty Trash from the Special menu
See what's in the Trash	Double-click on the Trash icon
Suppress Trash warnings	Hold down Option while you empty the Trash
Turn off Trash warnings	Select the Trash icon, press Command-I, and uncheck the Warn before emptying box
Eject a disk	Drag its icon to the Trash
Eject a disk but keep it in memory	Choose Eject from the Special menu or press Command-E
Copy a disk with only one floppy disk drive	Put the disk that's going to be the copy in the drive and eject it with Command-E; then insert the disk that you're copying and drag its icon over the dimmed icon of the first disk
Assign a color to an icon	Pick a color from the Color menu (unavailable if you don't have a color monitor)
Sort icons by color	Choose by color from the View menu
Create your own icon	Use a painting program and copy the image (Command-C); then open the icon's Get Info window (Command-I), select the icon, and paste the new one (Command-V)

What Else Is New?

There are a lot of new features in System 7 that don't quite rate a whole chapter of their own, but they're so important that you really ought to know what and where they are. So I'll put them all in this chapter, and it'll just be a hodgepodge of a lot of neat new features, like how to *find things*, what the mysterious aliases are, how to customize your Apple menu, and how to use labels and stationery pads.

System 7 makes it really easy to find what you're looking for, even if you've forgotten what you called it, whether it's a folder, a document, or a program. The Find command's now on the File menu, replacing the old Find File desk accessory. When you choose it (Command-F is the keyboard shortcut), you'll see a dialog box like this one.

Finding Things

▶ **Tip:** *The Find command is so good now that I use it to find everything, even if I know where it is, instead of clicking through a lot of folders, because it takes me right to what I'm looking for.*
...and if you think Find was good in 7.1, you should see it in 7.5! You can open documents, copy, and make aliases from its Find File Results box.

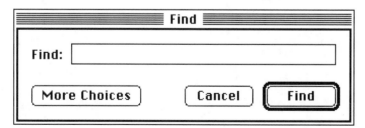

Don't be deceived by its simple look. This thing is a real powerpack.

If you know the name of what you're looking for, just type it in the Find box (use all lowercase letters if you're not sure how you capitalized it originally). When you click OK, the Mac will search your hard disk for the first occurrence of whatever you typed, even if it's only part of a name. When it finds it, it highlights it and shows you where it is. If it can't find it, you'll get a message.

▶ **Tip:** *Press Command-G to look again.*

If what it found isn't what you're looking for, you can look for the next one with the Find Again command. (Command-G is the keyboard shortcut).

Click More Choices to see what this feature can really do. Now suppose you want to find all the documents that have Rob (or rob) in their names. Just check the all at once button, and Commander Find will find all of them for you.

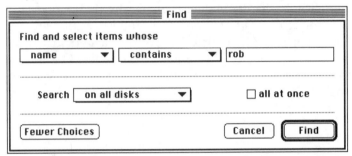

▶ **Tip:** *Find even searches your shared folders, too, if you're on a network.*

He'll even locate items in different folders for you. If you're searching all at once for something that's in several different folders, you'll be shown the first folder that's got what you're looking for and then be told to search again because there are more occurrences of that item in different folders.

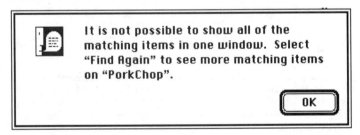

You can search for anything that's *contained* in a name, like searching for *rob* for folders, documents, and programs that have Roberta, Robert, robbing, and so forth in their names. Or—and here it gets neat—you can look for anything that *starts* a name, or *ends* a name, or that's NOT in a name. If you have the slightest clue as to what something's called, you can find it.

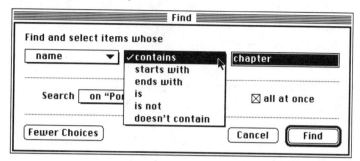

It's not just document names you can search for. You can search for documents that you've locked, or documents whose comments contain (or don't contain) something, or files whose size is less than or greater than so many kilobytes, or search by date of creation or by the date you last changed a document, or even go hunting for programs by their version number (even earlier and later versions). Now that's what I call service.

Just click on any of the choices that have a downward-pointing arrowhead next to them to see how else you can plan your search. Fewer Choices takes you back to the plain vanilla Find dialog box.

If you click on the Search box, you can choose whether to search all your disks, just the desktop (if that choice isn't dimmed), just your hard disk, just a floppy disk that you've inserted, just what's in the active window, or only the folders that you've selected.

Fine point: "On" searches on a disk and its desktop; "inside" searches the active window. This can be confusing if you're displaying the contents of a disk in the active window. If you search "inside" it, Find won't look at items that are out on the desktop.

When Find finds what it's looking for, if you're searching all at once, all the icons that meet your criteria

Tip: *If you don't want to search the whole hard disk but just the active window, use the Search pop-up menu and choose the name of the window*

Tip: *Check the all at once box to find everything that has what you're looking for.*

Tip: *One limitation of Find: it doesn't search your System file, so it won't locate fonts and sounds for you.*

Tip: *When Find has found several items, drag them all at once to the desktop by dragging just one of them. Use Put Away (Command-Y) to put them back in the right folders.*

will be highlighted. Here's a tip: instead of scrolling through a big window to see them, drag them all out to the desktop by dragging *just one* of them. You can then see which ones they are and use the Put Away command (Command-Y) to send them back to where they came from if they aren't what you want.

If you double-click on one of them while they're selected, you'll open all of them (if you've got enough memory).

Searching for files by modification date makes it easy to see which ones you need to back up. Searching by creation date lets you see which files are hopelessly outdated.

You can search by all the things listed here. To selectively search, look for items that meet one set of criteria and then narrow the search when you find them. Suppose you have a lot of files that have Tom in their names and you want to find those that were modified after a certain date. Easy. First, search for all files named Tom all at once. Since the items found are

> **Tip:** *You can search by Kind to locate all your alias files or all your programs. Or search by Lock to find all the files you've locked.*

```
✓name
 size
 kind
 label
 date created
 date modified
 version
 comments
 lock
```

selected, then choose More Choices and search just on the selected items for those whose date modified is after the date you choose. Today's date will be shown. To change it, just click on it and then retype the date, or click on the arrowheads next to it.

Aliases

MacDraw alias

Another hot new feature of System 7 is that it lets you make **aliases**. Unlike your nickname, the Mac's aliases are icons that substitute for the real thing. Here's how they work.

Suppose you have a program that you use a lot, but it's several folders down on your hard disk, and you have good reasons for keeping it there. Instead of opening folders to find it and then double-clicking on it to start it, with System 7 you can make an alias of it and keep it anywhere you like—even in the Apple menu, where you can get to it easily, or in the Startup Items folder, where it'll be started when you start your Mac.

You can make aliases of documents, folders, and disks, too. This lets you organize your work in several different ways. Want to keep your files by client *and* by month? Go ahead. File your invoices by customer *and* by project? Sure. Just make aliases of the documents you use a lot and put them in the folders where you'd expect to find them.

An alias isn't the same thing as the item itself; it's just a link or pointer to where the item can be found. That's why there aren't tiny triangles next to aliases in directory lists. When you double-click on them to open them, they'll just take you back to where the real thing is stored.

You can delete an alias icon, and the program or folder or document or disk won't be deleted from your computer. Also, when you move an alias, its original item stays right where it is: it doesn't move. But if you move the original item, the alias will find it. Even if you move it to another disk.

Which leads us to this trick. To save disk space on your hard disk, you can create aliases for things you've stored on floppy disks. When you open the alias on your hard disk, you'll be told which disk you need to insert to get it.

Tip: *Put aliases of programs you use a lot in the Apple Menu Items folder or out on the desktop so that you can find them and start them in a hurry. Put aliases of programs or documents that you want to start up with in the Startup Items folder.*

Tip: *For a quick way to make an alias in System 7.5 after you've found a file you were searching for, press Command and drag the file from the Find File Results box to the desktop. Instant alias!*

Tip: *If you find that you're often adding things or removing things from your Apple menu, here's a trick: Make an alias of the Apple Menu Items folder and keep it out on your desktop.*

Tip: *Dragging a file into an alias of a folder puts the file in the original folder.*

Tip: *Since aliases don't take up much space, you can have lots of them. And you can have more than one alias of the same thing.*

If you decide to use aliases for outdated files, be sure to give your disks unique names, or you may still have to go hunting through all the disks you've left named "Untitled" or "blank."

▶ **Tip:** *Want to make aliases of all your programs all at once? Use the Find command to search all at once for everything whose kind contains "application." Then choose Make Alias to make aliases for them all. The aliases will all be selected, so you can drag them to a folder, and you'll have a folder full of aliases of all your programs. Neat, and fast!*

Think about how great this is for a minute. No more hunting for outdated documents! I have eight little floppy disk file boxes lined up next to my Mac, and they're full of old, outdated files. If I had made a few aliases for some of those that I thought I might be looking for again, I'd save myself a lot of time flipping through the disks and reading disk labels.

If you work on a network, you can make aliases of your file servers or the documents that are stored on them so that you can quickly connect to them. See the Netiquette chapter for details.

To make an alias, select the item and then choose Make Alias from the Edit menu. You'll see a new icon with the item's name in italics (that's how you can tell alias icons: they're always in italics). If you want to give the alias a different name, fine. It's still what it is, no matter what you call it, because that pointer points back to the real thing. Then drag your alias icon to wherever you want it to be—in another folder, out on the desktop, wherever you like.

```
┌─────────────────────────────────────┐
│ ▤☐▤▤▤▤▤  xyz alias Info  ▤▤▤▤▤        │
│                                      │
│    ┌───┐                             │
│    │   │    xyz alias                │
│    └───┘                             │
│     Kind: alias                      │
│     Size: 1K on disk (502 bytes used)│
│                                      │
│    Where: PorkChop:                  │
│                                      │
│                                      │
│   Created: Sat, Apr 20, 1991, 9:48 AM│
│  Modified: Sat, Apr 20, 1991, 9:48 AM│
│  Original: ch 1 art : xyz            │
│                                      │
│                                      │
│  Comments:                           │
│  ┌────────────────────────────────┐  │
│  │                                │  │
│  │                                │  │
│  │                                │  │
│  └────────────────────────────────┘  │
│                                      │
│  ☐ Locked       ( Find Original )    │
└─────────────────────────────────────┘
```

To make a bunch of alias icons all at once, make the first one and then duplicate it with the Find menu's Duplicate command. But yes, you can make an alias of an alias if you want to.

You can lock an alias, but that just stops the alias from being thrown away. It doesn't lock the original file.

Sometimes nothing may happen when you open an alias. This can happen if you delete the original file from your disk. Your Mac can figure out what happened, though: just select the alias icon and choose Get Info. Click Find Original to see where the original is. You'll probably have to make the alias again.

◀ **Tip:** *Deleting the original file doesn't delete its aliases!*

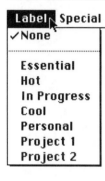

Using Labels

There's a new menu called the Label menu in System 7. What it does is let you assign a label to an icon. That's not the same thing as giving an icon a name. The label only shows when you look at a list of what's on a disk in any way *except* by icon or by small icon.

If you've got a color monitor, you can assign a color to a label so that all the icons that have that label will show up in that color, too.

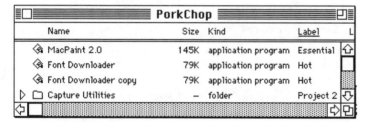

So how does this help you? Well, you can group related documents together with labels. Say you've got a project that has spreadsheets, graphics, and text created by three different programs. You can label them and then use the Find command to search for them all by label.

◀ **Tip:** *You use the Labels control panel to choose the text and colors for the Label menu.*

Stationery Pads (Templates)

bank letter

Another neat thing you can do with System 7 is turn a standard document that you've slaved over getting just right into a **stationery pad**. (These are also called **templates**.) All the formatting that you put into the document will be kept, along with the text, so if you're doing invoices, forms, standard contracts, or other kinds of boilerplate documents, turning each one into a stationery pad is great. (Of course, you could also do this before by just opening the original document and editing it for each new use, but if you're like me, you let your fingers do the walking and hit Command-S once too often and saved the thing with the new changes you made to it, which of course ruined it as a template.)

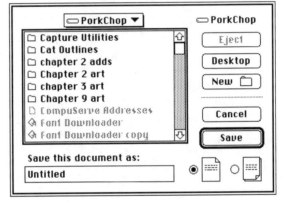

Click on the button next to the stack of paper to make a stationery pad, or check the Stationery pad box in the Get Info window

A lot of programs will have this feature built in. If they do, you'll see tiny stationery pad icons in the program's Save As dialog box (this one's from TeachText).

Click on the one that looks like a stack of papers to save the document as a stationery pad; then save the document.

Even if your program doesn't have a stationery pad option, you can turn a document into a stationery pad by using the Finder's Get Info box (Command-I). Choose the document and then choose Get Info. Then just click the Stationery pad box and close the window.

The document's icon then looks like a stationery pad. You can double-click on it to open it. If you've created it through the Finder, you'll be asked to give the new document a name when you open it, but if you've created it in your program, an untitled document will open, and you'll name it when you save it.

At Ease and System 7

If you're using a Performa, you're running an easy-to-use version of System 7 called System 7. *(whatever)* P. This simplified System 7 has an Application Launcher that lets inexperienced users start programs easily. A default document folder stores all the documents that are created, so you don't have to go looking for them. Another difference is that you're not aware of the "layers" of programs that are running—you just switch to the Finder or to another program by clicking on the Application menu.

System 7P also comes with an application named At Ease, which lets you decide which programs and documents are accessible on your Macintosh. You can purchase At Ease from Apple and use it on "regular" System 7 (any variety), too.

At Ease replaces the regular Finder with a much simpler and safer-to-use interface. There's no Trash, for example, so things can't get deleted by mistake. You have only two folders, one for programs and another one for documents, so everything's easy to find. You click once, not twice, to open items, so everything's easy to use. A Mouse Practice tutorial, complete with animation and sound, teaches how to use the mouse. You as system ad-

◀ **Tip:** *With System 7.5, you can set up your Finder to work much like a Performa. You can use a Launcher and a documents folder and stay in whatever program you're using even if you happen to click on the desktop. These features make the Finder easier for new users.*

ministrator (with At Ease 2.0) can set up passwords for groups and individuals and create personal setups of who gets to use which programs and documents. It's excellent for use in a classroom setting or for whenever new users have access to your Mac.

At Ease and the Performa's System 7P both make your Macintosh extremely easy to use, but there's one important difference between them. You don't need a Performa to run At Ease.

The At Ease 2.0 interface

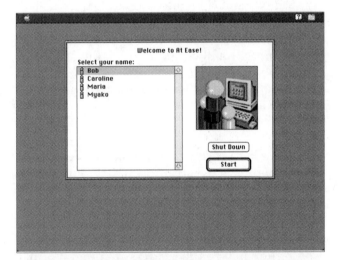

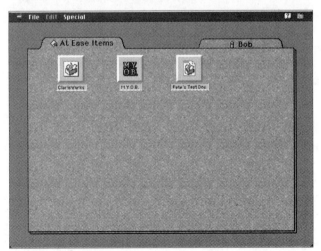

Starting Programs and Opening Documents

The most important thing you do with your Mac is run programs on it. The Finder and all the other bells and whistles don't do you much good unless you can run a word processing program, a spreadsheet, a graphics program, a few games, whatever.

Installing Programs

The very first thing you ought to do when you buy a program and tear off the shrink wrap is to lock the disk so that you or anybody else can't change what's on it. To lock a disk, open the write-protect hole. Then, it's a good idea to make copies of the disks and put the originals away in a safe place. Use the duplicates to put the program on your hard disk; that way you'll know right away if the copies you made are good.

If your program doesn't come with an Installer, you can copy it onto your hard disk by dragging the disk icon of the program onto the icon of your hard disk. It's a good idea, though, to double-click on the program disk icon first and see what folders are on it and what's in them. You may not want or need everything that's there, like *another* copy of TeachText or a bunch of Read Mes (you can just read them from the floppy disk and not copy them unless you really need them). You'll also probably want to create a folder for your program and its files on your hard disk and drag the program disk icon onto that folder. Or you can just drag selected files from the program disk into whatever folders you like on your hard disk.

◀ **Tip:** *Many programs that you buy nowadays, especially if they come on several disks, have their own Installer. Use it.*

One thing to keep in mind (it can't be said often enough) is: don't copy the System Folder, if there's one on your program floppy disk, onto your hard disk. More than one System Folder per disk can cause problems. But System Folders have gotten so big lately that there's little chance of this happening. In fact, System 7's too big to fit on a regular (800K) floppy disk. But you could copy an earlier System Folder by mistake. Just be aware of the possibility.

▶ **Tip:** *See page 52 for a trick for making aliases of all your programs all at once.*

Once you've copied the program onto your hard disk, you may want to make a few aliases for it and put them in choice locations, like the Apple menu, where they're easy to get at. It all depends on how often you're planning to use the program and whether it's going to be one of your basic applications or just one that you use on rainy days.

Starting Programs

To start a program, double-click on its icon. (You can also select it and choose Open from the File menu if you like.) These aren't the only ways, though. You can also start a program by double-clicking on a document that was created in it, or by dragging a document icon onto the program's icon. This last trick is new in System 7, and it can let you open a document in a program that didn't create it, like a text-only document in a word processing program, without having to open the program first. If the program can open it, it'll highlight when you drag the document onto it.

▶ **Tip:** *If a program's icon is grayed, it's already open. You can double-click on it to switch to it.*

MacWrite

Switching between Programs

Once you've started a couple or more programs, you can switch between them by clicking in one of their windows, if you can see part of one on the screen, or by choosing from the Application menu—the one that appears when you click the icon in the upper-right corner of the screen.

▶ **Tip:** *Being able to switch between programs makes it really easy to cut and paste between them, too.*

Each time you open another program, its name will be added to the list on the Application menu. A check mark next to a program's name indicates that it's the one that's currently active, and the icon you see is the one for that program, too.

Tip: *To go out to the desktop, click on the desktop pattern, if you can see it. Or choose Finder from the Application menu.*

If a program's icon in the Application menu is dimmed, it means that its windows have been hidden. You can choose it from the list, and it'll quickly open again. (It's still in memory.)

Hiding Windows

You can hide all the windows you've got open except those that belong to the program you're in. This is great if your screen is getting so cluttered that you can't tell where you are. Just choose Hide Others from the Application menu. You can hide the windows of the active program, too. That will show you just the Finder, if you've hidden the others.

To see all the windows again, choose (you guessed it) Show All.

Tip: *Press Option as you choose another program from the Application menu, and the program you were working in will be hidden. Press Option and click on the desktop to hide all application windows.*

Starting Another Program

To start another program, go out to the Finder (you can just click on the desktop, if you can see it, or use the Application menu if you can't) and double-click on the program's icon, or open one of its documents using one of the tricks we talked about earlier.

If you get a "not enough memory" message, you've run out of RAM. You'll need to close a program to start a new one. Go to the program and Quit from it. Hiding or closing its windows won't do it; the program stays in memory when you do that.

Tip: *To see how much memory your programs are using, go out to the Finder and choose About This Macintosh from the Apple menu. When Balloon Help is on, you'll see a message about how much memory each program is actually using if you point at the graphs.*

Lost? Use the Application Menu

Sometimes you can get lost if you're running a program but it doesn't have a window open. You see a strange-looking menu at the top of the screen, and you know it's not the Finder, but what is it? Click on the handy Application menu to find out. (TeachText does this to me all the time, with its tiny little menu bar.)

Background Copying

Another neat thing that System 7 lets you do is make copies of files while you're working in a program. To do this, go out to the Finder and start the copy process. As soon as the copying starts, go back to your program and keep on working. You won't be able to start another program running until the copying is done, but who cares? This is a real time-saver.

Background Printing

If you're printing on a LaserWriter, you can continue to work on your programs while it prints your documents. Make sure that Background printing is On in the Chooser. See Chapter 7 for details.

Opening Documents

Want to open a bunch of documents at the same time? Easy. Just Shift-click or drag-select to select them in the Finder and then double-click on *one of* them.

If the documents are created by different programs, hey, no problem (as long as you've got enough memory). System 7 will start the programs running and open the documents, too.

To locate a document that you're looking for, don't forget the hidden pop-up menu that you can get at by holding down the Command key and clicking on the window's title in the Finder. You can go to different levels of folders this way. To close a window while you move to a new level, hold down the Option key (you've already got the Command key down) while you select the new folder.

If you're within a program, you open documents by using the Open command on the File menu (Command-O is the keyboard shortcut). This brings up a System 7-style

▶ **Tip:** *To create a brand new document, use your program's New command (Command-N).*

▶ **Tip:** *Pop-up menus are like pull-down menus, but they aren't in the menu bar. If you see a downward-pointing arrowhead, it's leading to a pop-up menu.*

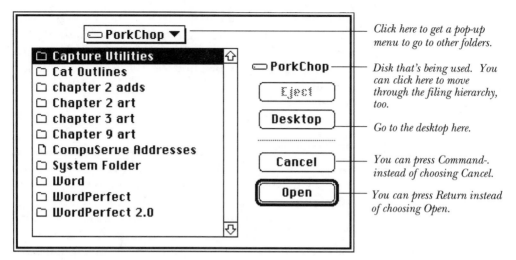

Click here to get a pop-up menu to go to other folders.

Disk that's being used. You can click here to move through the filing hierarchy, too.

Go to the desktop here.

You can press Command-. instead of choosing Cancel.

You can press Return instead of choosing Open.

directory dialog box. It's a little different from the old ones (see the one above). Here are a few tricks for using it.

See the folder icon at the top with the downward-pointing arrowhead? Clicking on it pops up a menu showing you all the folders that lead to the folder you're in. "Desktop" will be at the bottom. You can go to another folder by dragging and releasing on its name.

Click on Desktop to see what's out on the desktop. This is also how to get to another disk. If the document you're looking for isn't on the floppy disk in the drive, click Eject to switch floppy disks.

◀ **Tip:** *Click on Desktop to see what's on other disks.*

When you see the document you want, just double-click on it. You can click on Open or press Return, too, but double-clicking is faster.

Remember, the document you're looking for may be inside another folder, and you may need to open several folders to find it.

◀ **Tip:** *Just type the first few letters of a document's name to go to it quickly in a list. When it's highlighted, you can just press Return to open it.*

Unfortunately, System 7.1 doesn't remember what you looked at last and take you back there the next time you want to open another document. However, System 7.5 lists Recent Documents and Recent Applications (as well as Recent Servers) on the Apple menu, and you can choose the ones you worked with lately from here. You can also specify that the folder you saved in last be opened the next time you save, or specify one folder for saving

And another beef: because of the way computers do

numbers, if the document you're looking for begins with a number, it can get downright tedious to scroll through a window to find 5-22 or 6-41. But here's how to get around that: just type the number, and the Mac will take you right to it, and you can press Return to open it without even having to reach for your mouse.

Saving Documents

To save the document you're working on, choose Save from the program's File menu (Command-S is its shortcut.) If you've already saved a document, to save it under a different name, in a different folder or on a different disk, or out on the desktop, use the Save As command instead. There's no keyboard shortcut for it (but you can make one with a utility like QuicKeys[2] from CE Software, 515-224-1995).

The Save As dialog box is different in System 7. (If you haven't saved a document yet, you see the Save As dialog box when you choose Save.) Like the Open dialog box you saw earlier, it has new buttons. One lets you create a new folder to save the document in, and the other lets you zip out to the desktop, where you can switch disks.

▶ **Tip:** *If you want two copies of a document in the same folder, one of them will have to have a different name. You can't use the same name in the same folder.*

▶ **Tip:** *Save often. Enough said.*

Getting to the Desktop
To get to the very top of your filing system, click on the Desktop button or choose Desktop from the pop-up menu. Remember, the desktop holds the Trash, disks, file servers, and anything else you've put there so that you can find it quickly.

Saving a Document on Another Disk
Once you're at the Desktop level, you'll see any other disks that you've put in your disk drive listed. Just choose the one you want to save the document onto, or eject the one that's there and insert a different disk.

Quitting from Programs

Usually you exit from a program by choosing Quit (Command-Q) from its File menu. To close all the programs you've got running without having to quit from each one individually, go out to the Finder (use the Application menu) and choose Shut Down. You'll be asked whether you want to save any changes that you haven't saved yet.

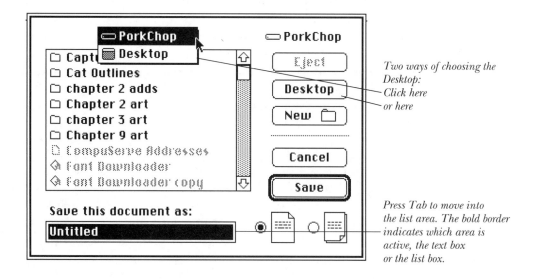

Two ways of choosing the Desktop:
Click here
or here

Press Tab to move into the list area. The bold border indicates which area is active, the text box or the list box.

Publish and Subscribe

Another new feature in System 7 is that you can automatically update your documents. It's also called **live** or **dynamic cutting and pasting**. As you make changes in the original document, they'll automatically be made in the other documents, too.

If your program will let you do dynamic cutting and pasting, you'll see commands like Create Publisher and Subscribe to in your Edit menu. What you do is select the material that you want to be able to automatically update—text, graphics, database information, whatever. This material is called the **publisher**. (It's just the selected material, not the whole document, that's the publisher.) You choose Create Publisher from the Edit menu and give the it a name. This saves it in a separate file that's called an **edition**. You can open this file to see what's in it, but you can't change it. To change it, you have to go back to the original publisher in the original file.

After you've created an edition, you can put it in as many documents as you like. They're your **subscribers**. Say you've got part of a spreadsheet or a graph of the data

◀ **Tip:** *If you don't have Pubs and Subs in your programs, you can always move things from one program to another via the Clipboard.*

in a spreadsheet that you want to put in a few different reports. Open the document that you want the material to be automatically updated in, click to set an insertion point, and choose Subscribe To from the program's Edit menu. You'll see a directory dialog box. Choose the edition you want, and it'll be put in your document. A gray border will be around it so that you can tell it from the rest of your document. If it's not exactly where you want it, you can cut and paste it to get it in the right location.

There are a lot of options you can use with publishers and subscribers, but they're different in different programs, so take a look at your program's manual (I hate to say that, but there's no help for it) to see what yours can do. You may be able to see the date and time that an edition was updated, for example, and you'll probably be able to choose between automatic and manual updates. If you're working on a network and sharing documents, you'll find this feature really valuable. See the Netiquette chapter for more on networking.

System 7's Publish and Subscribe feature can change the way you work, if you're part of a workgroup. System 7.5's PowerTalk can change the way you work in a workgroup even more. It gives you a universal mailbox where you can receive all your mail—faxes, Internet mail, CompuServe mail, even voice mail (with telephone applications) and lets you electronically "sign" your documents and unlock access to your network with one password. See Chapter 12 for more about PowerTalk and how to use its AppleMail.

Put a new program on your hard disk	Drag its icon to your hard disk's icon (better make a new folder first)	**Techniques and Shortcuts for Working with Documents**
Start a program	Double-click on its icon, or select it and choose Open from the File menu (Command-O), or drag a document icon over a program's icon and "drop" it	
Open a document in the Finder	Double-click on its icon, or select it and choose Open from the File menu (Command-O), or drag a document icon over a program's icon and "drop" it	
Open several documents from the Finder	Select them and double-click on one of them	
Open a document in a program	Choose Open from the File menu (Command-O) and use the directory dialog box. Click on the folder at the top or the disk icon to move through the levels of folders	
Create a new document	Choose New from the a program's File menu (Command-N)	
See which folders you're in	Command-click in a Finder window's title; in an Open or Save As dialog box, click on the pop-up menu at the top or on the tiny disk icon	
Close a Finder window and move to a new level	Hold down the Option key while you choose a new folder	

Open a document on another disk	Choose Open from the File menu (Command-O) and click on Desktop; then choose the disk (eject it if you need to insert another)
Switch between programs you've started	Click in a window of the program you want, or choose its name from the Application menu
Hide windows of all but the active program	Choose Hide Others from the Application menu
Show all windows, even hidden ones	Choose Show All from the Application menu
Go to the desktop	Click on the desktop pattern, if you can see it, or choose Desktop from an Open or Save As dialog box, or choose Finder from the Application menu, or press Command-Shift-Up arrow in a Finder window
Start another program	Go to the desktop and double-click on its icon or open one of its documents
Copy while you're working	Go to the desktop and start the copy process; then return to the program you were working in
Save a document	Choose Save from the File menu (Command-S)
Save a document under a different name, in another folder, on another disk, or out on the desktop	Use the Save As command in the File menu
Create a new folder to save a document in	Click on New Folder in a Save As dialog box

Quit from your programs	Choose Quit from the File menu (Command-Q) or choose Shut Down from the Finder's Special menu
See how much memory a program's using	Choose About This Macintosh from the Apple menu
Publish material	Select it and choose Create Publisher from a program's Edit menu
Subscribe to published material	Click to set an insertion point and choose Subscribe To from the program's Edit menu

Control Panels

6

Control panels (they're plural now) let you customize how your Mac looks and acts. Some come with System 7, and you can buy others. With the ones that come with System 7, you can change the "feel" of the mouse, let network users have access to your Mac or lock them out in the cold, pick a different beep sound, set yourself up to use the keyboard instead of the mouse, view a world map and check the local time, and change the pattern and color of the desktop, just to give a few examples.

System 7 handles your Mac's control panel differently from the way earlier Systems did. Instead of control panel files being "loose" in the System Folder, there's now a Control Panels folder, which is itself in the System Folder. And instead of having just one control panel, you have many. To add a new control panel to your system, you just drag its icon into the Control Panels folder. Or drag it to the System Folder and let the Mac figure out where to put it.

You can get at your control panels to set them in three different ways:

- Choose Control Panels from the Apple menu and then choose a control panel
- Double-click on a control panel icon in the Control Panels folder (it's in the System Folder)
- Double-click on the Control Panels alias in the Apple Menu Items folder and then pick a control panel.

You'll get a separate dialog box for each different control panel.

Control Panels

◀ **Tip:** *The control panels you can use depend on which model of Macintosh you have. You can buy others from software manufacturers. They're also called cdevs, for control panel devices.*

◀ **Tip:** *You can just drag icons into the System Folder and System 7 will usually be able to decide which folder they belong in. (It'll ask if this is OK with you first.)*

```
┌─────────────────────────────────────────────────────────────┐
│ ▤▢▨▨▨▨▨▨▨▨▨▨ Control Panels ▨▨▨▨▨▨▨▨ ▣▤ │
│   ┌──────────────────────────────────────────────────────┐   │
│   │  Name                        Size    Kind            │   │
│   ├──────────────────────────────────────────────────┬───┤   │
│   │  ▢ Color                     12K   control panel  │⇧ │   │
│   │  ▢ Date & Time               35K   control panel  │  │   │
│   │  ▢ Easy Access               12K   control panel  │  │   │
│   │  ▢ Extensions Manager        27K   control panel  │  │   │
│   │  ▢ File Sharing Monitor       4K   control panel  │  │   │
│   │  ▢ General Controls          22K   control panel  │  │   │
│   │  ▢ Keyboard                   8K   control panel  │  │   │
│   │  ▢ Labels                     3K   control panel  │  │   │
│   │  ▢ Map                       30K   control panel  │  │   │
│   │  ▢ Memory                    38K   control panel  │  │   │
│   │  ▢ Monitors                  40K   control panel  │  │   │
│   │  ▢ MountImage                10K   control panel  │  │   │
│   │  ▢ Mouse                      8K   control panel  │  │   │
│   │  ▢ Numbers                   16K   control panel  │  │   │
│   │  ▢ Sharing Setup              4K   control panel  │  │   │
│   │  ▢ Sound                     17K   control panel  │  │   │
│   │  ▢ Startup Disk               5K   control panel  │  │   │
│   │  ▢ Users & Groups             4K   control panel  │⇩ │   │
│   └──────────────────────────────────────────────────┴───┘   │
│   ⇦                                                  ⇨       │
└─────────────────────────────────────────────────────────────┘
```

There are all kinds of different control panels now

▽ ▢ Apple Menu Items

    🖇 Alarm Clock

    🖇 Calculator

    🖇 Chooser

    ▢ *Control Panels*

    🖇 Key Caps

    🖇 Note Pad

    🖇 Puzzle

    🖇 Scrapbook

▶ **Tip:** *If you use a control panel a lot, make an alias for it and put it in the Apple menu by itself, or put it out on your desktop. Leave the original in the Control Panels folder to avoid trouble.*

Some of the old control panels, like Keyboard, have new features. And there are lots of new control panels, like Labels, Views, Users & Groups, and Sharing Setup. Startup Items replaces the old Set Startup command that used to be on the Special menu. It lets you choose which programs to open at startup. And Memory gives you a new way to set a disk cache, which is a trick for setting aside memory for routine operations.

Your Desktop

There are all kinds of things you can do to personalize your desktop. A lot of folks use their Macs for years without exploring some these. Now is the time to test them out, while you're getting used to the new system.

General Controls

This control panel lets you change your desktop pattern (and color, if you've got a color monitor). It also lets you set the rate that the menus and the insertion point blink, and set the date, time, and the time format.

General Controls

Changing the Desktop Pattern and Color

Your Mac comes with several preset desktop patterns. To see them and look at a preview of what they'll look like on your desktop, click on the arrows above the desktop pattern in the General Controls panel. When you see one you like, click on the tiny desktop under the arrows.

◀ **Tip:** *System 7.5 has a much-changed General Controls panel plus over 50 desktop patterns to choose from. See Chapter 11.*

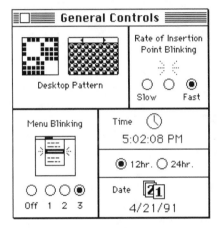

◀ **Tip:** *Several? Many. I stopped clicking at 25 and I still hadn't seen all of them yet. You get a lot more patterns on a black-and-white monitor, but you get color patterns on a color monitor.*

You can edit these patterns pixel by pixel in the little window to the left of the desktop. Just click with the mouse on a black spot to turn it white, and vice versa.

To change a color in a pattern, double-click on the color in the color bar and then pick a new color from the color wheel.

To get a solid color, click on a color in the color bar and drag the pointer all over the pattern. Or double-click on a color, use the color wheel to change it, and then color your pattern.

◀ **Tip:** *If you don't click on the tiny desktop, your big desktop pattern won't change.*

▲**Warning:** *Double-click on the little desktop to save the pattern when you've got the pattern as you like it. Otherwise you'll lose it the next time you display another pattern.*

Changing the Blink Rate

You can also change whether the menu items blink when you choose them, and how many times they blink. They're preset to blink three times.

The insertion point blinks, too, and you can choose whether it's slow or fast. You'll see a demo of how it looks when you click the 1, 2, or 3 buttons.

Setting the Date and Time

▶ **Tip:** *You can choose 12-hour format or 24-hour format for the time.*

Your Mac has a clock and calendar that run continuously. To reset the clock (which you'll have to do twice a year for Daylight Savings time), click on the hour, minute, or second that you want to change. (You have to change them one by one.) You'll see two scroll arrows appear next to it. Click on those to set the time, or just retype what you've selected.

 **Alarm Clock**

You can also use the Alarm Clock desk accessory in the Apple menu to set the time. You click on the tiny icon that looks like a taxi meter flag or a musical note and then click on the wall clock icon.

The Alarm Clock also lets you set an alert time, to warn yourself when it's meeting time, for instance. Click on the little flag icon and then the alarm clock. The time that you see is the current alarm clock setting. You can change it to whatever you want and then click the little icon that looks like a keyhole on the right to turn on the alarm clock. When the clock goes off, you'll hear a beep, and then the Apple menu icon will flash, alternating with the alarm clock icon. Click on the keyhole icon again to turn it off.

To change the date, click on the month, day, or year and then just retype what you've selected. You can also use the scroll arrows to change it.

Views

▶ **Tip:** *System 7.1 and 7.5 have different Date & Time control panels.*

This control panel lets you specify which font to use in Finder windows and whether you want icons on the screen to be aligned neatly in rows and columns or staggered, like on a checkerboard. It also lets you choose which information you want to be displayed in list views and how large you want small icons to be.

Views

Here's how a 12-point New York Finder window viewed by icon looks, using large icons and a staggered grid:

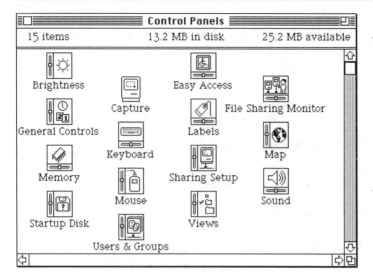

◀ **Tip:** *Choose a staggered grid if you use a larger point size or larger icons. That way you'll be able to read the names of the icons.*

◀ **Tip:** *Another control panel called CloseView (on the Tidbits disk) lets you enlarge what you're looking at. See the System Tools chapter for details.*

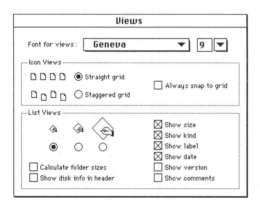

Numbers

PowerBook

If you have trouble reading the small type on the Mac's screen, experiment with this one until you get a combination that you like. If you choose a different grid arrangement, choose Clean Up Window from the Special menu to see how the icons line up.

◀ **Tip:** *System 7.1 adds two more control panels– Numbers for specifying number formats, and a new PowerBook control panel. System 7.5 adds many more new control panels, including several for PowerBooks. See Chapter 11.*

The font sizes that appear in outline form are the ones that look best on the screen, but you can type a number for the font size, too.

Check Calculate Folder Size if you want to see how much each folder holds. Also, checking Show disk info in header is handy for seeing how much room is left on a disk.

Labels

Labels

This feature is new in System 7. What it does is let you change the words and the colors that are on the Label menu. For example, if you wanted to label your files by projects named Jones, Smith, Hernandez, and so forth, you'd change the labels here to get them to appear on the Labels menu.

Labels
Peoria
Topeka
Santa Fe
Birmingham
Personal Papers
Final Reports
Estimates--Gordon Project

To change the colors (these are the colors used for the icons), click on a color and then pick a new one from the color wheel.

See Chapter 4 for more suggestions about how to use the Labels menu.

Sound

Sound

The Sound control panel lets you set the sound that's used for a beep and adjust its volume.

With System 7, sounds are in your System file, and you can click on a sound there to hear a sample of what it's like and how loud it will be played. You can do the same thing with this Sound control panel, and it also lets you turn up the decibels or hush your beep so that folks in the next cubicle won't know you're getting beeped at. If you turn the sound all the way down to 0, the menu bar will flash to alert you to what you'd normally get beeped for.

▶ **Tip:** *To add new sounds with System 7, just drag them to your System file in your System Folder.*

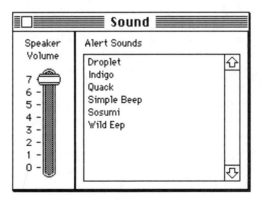

You can gets lots of sounds as freeware from most Mac electronic bulletin boards or from Mac forums on CompuServe or the other big information utilities. Or, if you don't have a modem and can't download files from bulletin boards, you can buy disks full of sounds from catalogs, like those from Somak Software (800-842-5020) and BMUG (call 415-540-1740 for a catalog).

▶ **Tip:** *You can also add sounds with MacRecorder from Farallon Computing (415-596-9100).*

Some Macs will let you record your own sounds if you connect a microphone to your computer. Once it's connected, open the Sound control panel and click Add. Then click Record, record your new sound (you've got ten seconds), and click Stop. To save the new sound, click Save and give it a name.

Startup Disk

This control panel lets you choose which disk to use as the startup disk, if you have more than one hard disk. The one you select will be used to start your computer until you select another one later.

Startup Disk

You need to use a floppy disk to start up your Mac when you install new system software. When you start your computer with a floppy disk in the drive (as long as it has a working System Folder on it), the Mac will use that disk as the startup disk. Since you can't install a new system (or upgrade to a newer version) on the disk that's in use as the startup disk, be sure to start up with the Installer disk.

Your Screen

Brightness

> **Tip:** *Use the Label menu to pick colors for icons.*

The Color and Brightness control panels let you customize how your screen looks, and Monitors lets you pick how many colors or shades of gray to display. You won't be able to use these control panels on some Macintoshes, but there are lots of other control panels that you can use.

To change the desktop pattern and colors, use General Controls. For a different number of colors on your Mac, it's Monitors. Use Color to change the color of window borders and highlighting. To change the color of icons? The Labels control panel.

Color

This one lets you select a color for highlighted text and window borders. (You can't set a different color if your monitor is displaying only black and white, though.) Choose Other... from the pop-up menu, and you'll see a color wheel (also called the Color Picker). Click on the color you want for the highlight. For duller colors, drag the scroll box down; for brighter, drag it up. Go wild.

> **Tip:** *Don't pick a deep color for your highlighting, or you won't be able to read text through it.*

```
┌─────────────────── Color ═══════════════╗
│ ☐ ▤▤▤▤▤                                  │
│                                          │
│  Highlight color:    ┌─ Other...    ▼ ─┐ │
│  ▐Sample text▐                           │
│                                          │
│  Window color:       ┌─ Red         ▼ ─┐ │
│                                          │
└──────────────────────────────────────────┘
```

When you click on another color, you'll see a sample of how it looks, and the former highlight color will be underneath it.

You can also pick a color for your Finder window borders. Open the pop-up menu and pick one. You'll instantly see the results in the active window.

Brightness

Brightness

The Brightness control panel lets you set the brightness of the screen. It's available only on some Macs. If your Mac doesn't let you use this control panel, reach under the Apple logo on the front of your computer (for built-in monitors) or around behind the right side of the screen (for separate monitors). There should be a dial there that will let you change the brightness.

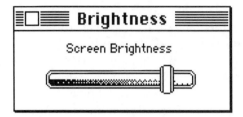

You can buy a screen saver utility like After Dark (from Berkeley Systems, 415-540-5535) to keep interesting patterns and messages your screen. They don't really "save" screens any more, but screen savers are fun.

Monitors

You'll use this one to change the number of shades of gray or colors your screen displays. If you have more than one monitor, you also use it to set which is the main monitor.

Changing the Number of Colors

You can set how many colors or shades of gray you want your monitor to display—if you have that kind of monitor. If you don't, the Mac won't show you the Monitors control panel anyway. With System 7.5, you can change your monitor's resolution on the fly; the Monitors control panel has been improved.

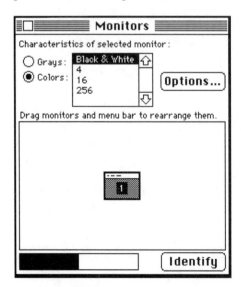

Just click on the number of colors you want to use. Your display will immediately change to show you the effect. Next to the Identify button, you'll see all the possible colors. (If you're wondering what that button does, it identifies which monitor is which if you have more than one.)

If your Mac can handle built-in video, you can also use the Monitors control panel to set aside memory to use for video. See your *Special Features* booklet about this one.

Changing the Startup Monitor

▶ **Tip:** *Choose your largest monitor as your startup monitor.*

If you have two or more monitors, you can change which one's to be used as the main startup monitor. Just drag the menu bar to the monitor that you want to be the main one. The monitor icon with the menu bar on it indicates the main monitor.

Showing the Monitor's Positions

▶ **Tip:** *You'll need to restart your computer for monitor changes to take effect.*

With two monitors, you'll sometimes need to tell your Mac where they are in relation to each other so that the pointer can move from one to another. Select the icon of the one you want to move and drag it to its new relative location. (Make sure the icons touch.) None of this is going to make any sense to you if you don't have two monitors.

Your Mouse and Keyboard

The Mac wouldn't be the Mac if it didn't offer you a lot of choices. You can customize your mouse and keyboard, too. You can even set your computer up so that you don't have to use the mouse at all. Most folks will probably want to use the mouse for some things and not for others, but some aren't so lucky and don't have that choice. If you can tap a key, you can use a Mac. I always wondered what Easy Access was before writing this book. Now I know: it's basically for the physically challenged, and I'm really impressed with the thought Apple put into its design so that Macintoshes could indeed be used by almost all of the rest of us.

Mouse

Mouse

You use the Mouse control panel to adjust the "feel" of the mouse. This is called **mouse tracking**, and it's the relation between how far you move the mouse on your real desk-top and how far the mouse pointer moves on the screen. If you set it to Fast, the pointer will go twice as fast as the mouse. I like mine set to Fast because it lets me "scootch" the mouse over my desktop without lifting my wrist off the desk, in a series of little sweeps. Try this and see if you like it. This method has saved many a cup of coffee from get-ting dumped.

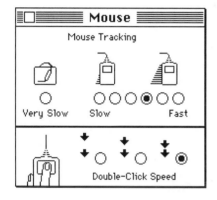

◀ **Tip:** *Pick Very Slow if you're drawing with the mouse.*

◀ **Tip:** *Set the Speed to Fast if you're short on space on your real desktop. You won't have to move the mouse as far.*

◀ **Tip:** *If you set the mouse to the middle or slow speed, you can still click faster. If you set it to the fastest speed, though, it won't recognize slow clicks as double-clicks.*

By the way, you can pick the mouse up and the pointer on the screen won't move. If you get dangerously near the edge of your desk and your arm just won't stretch any fur-ther... just pick the mouse up and put it down again. This may seem obvious to some of you but to many of us it's not. (Remember to keep the mouse button down if it was down before you picked up the mouse.)

The Double-Click Speed button lets you set the interval that the Mac interprets as a double click. Choose one and watch the finger on the left. The mouse will blink to show you a demo of that rate.

◀ **Tip:** *If your Mac interprets two clicks as a double-click, choose a faster setting.*

Keyboard

The Keyboard control panel lets you change the key re-peat rate—how fast a key repeats when you press and hold it down. Set it to Long if you have a "heavy" touch and you're getting extra characters as you're typing.

You can also change how sensitive the keyboard is to your touch by setting a different delay rate. If you set this to Off, keys *won't* repeat when you hold them down.

Keyboard

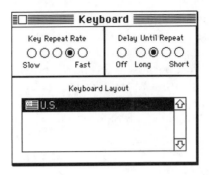

Keyboard Layout lets you specify a keyboard other than English. The French keyboard, for example, uses an AZERTY arrangement instead of the QWERTY layout on US keyboards. But depending on where you bought your Mac, you may have only one choice here anyway.

Easy Access

Easy Access

Easy Access lets you use the keys on the numeric keypad instead of using the mouse. It's designed for people who have problems with two-handed typing or using a mouse, but even if you don't have difficulty with these, Easy Access gives you more control over the movement of the pointer on the screen, which is handy for fine-tuning graphics, as you can move the pointer one pixel at a time.

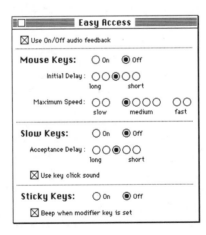

There are three things you can set with Easy Access: Mouse Keys lets you use the numeric keypad instead of the mouse, Sticky Keys lets you do one-handed typing in those cases where you need to press more than one key at once, and Slow Keys tells the Mac to wait just a bit before accepting a key press.

Mouse Keys for Moving the Pointer

With Mouse Keys, you can use the numeric keyboard instead of the mouse. To turn on Mouse Keys, press Command-Shift-Clear. (You can also turn it on by opening the Easy Access control panel, but if you can't use a mouse, it'll be hard to get at that control panel, right? So Apple has provided ways for turning these features on and off with the keyboard, too). You'll hear a rising tone to let you know Mouse Keys is turning on.

◀ **Tip:** *System 7 lets you scroll a window by dragging an icon to the top or bottom, or to one of its sides. Easy Access users take note: you can scroll this way, too.*

When Mouse Keys is on, pressing the 5 on the numeric keypad works like a mouse button. You press it once for a click and twice for a double-click.

To move the pointer, you use the keys around the 5 key: the 6 key (right), the 2 key (down), the 4 key (left), and the 8 key (up). Hold the key down to move the pointer quickly.

To lock the mouse button down so that you can drag, press the 0 key. To unlock the mouse button, press the decimal point key.

To turn off Mouse Keys, press Command-Shift-Clear again (you'll hear a falling tone), or click its button in the Easy Access control panel.

Slow Keys

Using Slow Keys gives you a little leeway in how the Mac interprets keystrokes. It waits just a bit before it accepts a key press as a keystroke. You can also choose whether you hear a click when you press the key. You can use both Slow Keys and Sticky Keys together if you have trouble typing.

Sticky Keys for One-Handed Typing

When Sticky Keys is on, you can type keys one by one that normally have to be typed all at the same time, like Command-P for Print. You can press Command and then press P.

▶ **Tip:** *When Sticky Keys is on, there's a tiny icon in the upper-right corner of the screen. Watch it closely.*

To turn on Sticky Keys from the keyboard, press the Shift key five times. Don't move the mouse. If you do, you'll have to start over. You'll hear a rising tone to indicate that it's turned on, and a little icon will appear in the upper right of your screen.

To use Sticky Keys once you've turned it on, press the modifier key that you want to use (like the Command, Option, Shift, or Control key; there's a Control key on the SE keyboard).

The little icon will change to let you know you've begun a key sequence. You'll also hear a beep, if you haven't unchecked the beep box for Sticky Keys in the Easy Access control panel.

▶ **Tip:** *Here's how to eject a floppy disk if you don't use a mouse: press Command-Shift-1 for the disk in the internal floppy disk drive and Command-Shift-2 for a disk in an external floppy drive.*

Press the rest of the keys that you need to complete the combination.

For example, to save the document you're working on, you'd press Command and S. You'll hear another beep to signal that it's done.

To lock a key, press it twice. The icon will change again, indicating that the key's locked. For example, to Shift-click with Sticky Keys and Mouse Keys so that you can select items that aren't next to each other, press Shift twice to lock it and press 5 to select the first item. Then move to the last item you want to select and press 5 again.

As long as that little icon's in the upper-right corner, Sticky Keys is on. To turn it off, press Shift five times again, or press any two of the Command, Option, Shift, or Control keys at the same time.

Special Features

A few new special control panels come with System 7. The world Map is worth exploring when you've got some free time.

Map

Map

The Map control panel lets you see the local time for just about anywhere on the globe, and you can use it to see where cities are, too. It's got some neat hidden tricks.

It's ideal if you've got a portable and you're flying from place to place, because you can set your current location, and it will adjust the time and date in your Mac for you.

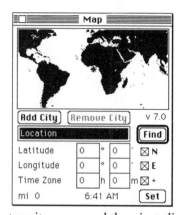

Finding a City

To locate a city, type its name and choose Find. If the name's in the Map, you'll see the city's location flash. If you want to see which cities are on the Map, hold down Option while you click Find. You'll cycle through the Map's list alphabetically.

> ◀ **Tip:** *Cities the Map knows about are represented by tiny dots.*

> ◀ **Tip:** *You don't have to type a city's complete name. Just type enough characters to get a match. This can help you find cities you're not sure how to spell.*

To add a city to the Map, type its name and then just click on its location and click Add City. You can enter its longitude and latitude, if you know them, instead of clicking on an approximate location.

You can scroll it sideways and up and down by putting the pointer on an edge of the Map and holding the mouse button down.

Checking the Time Difference

Click on the words "Time Zone" to see the difference in time between the last spot you clicked and the current location. The time zone shows the hours and minutes ahead of Greenwich Mean Time.

> ◀ **Tip:** *To get a closeup view, hold down the Option key when you open the Map.*

Color Maps

If you've got a color monitor, look in the Scrapbook. There's a color map. To change its colors, copy it and paste it in a painting program (like PixelPaint from SuperMac Technology, 408-245-2202, or some other), color it, and copy and paste it back in the Map control panel again.

> ◀ **Tip:** *The mileage shown on the map is the distance between the last spot you clicked and the current location. To reset it, click on Set.*

Memory

You can set a disk cache with the Memory control panel, which is just a fancy way of saying that you can specify a certain amount of memory for your Mac to use to hold information about the most recent things it's done on your disk, like going out and getting files and saving them. The size of the disk cache controls the number of programs you can work with at once. You might think that a bigger

Memory

disk cache means more programs, but that's not the way it works. Because a disk cache puts aside memory, the bigger the disk cache, the fewer programs you can run, because less memory is available to them.

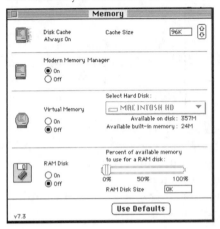

With System 7, you always have a disk cache that's pre-set to whatever's best for the type of Mac you have. If you want to work with a lot of programs but keep getting an out-of-memory message, set your disk cache smaller, like 32K or 64K. Click Use Defaults to reset it to the factory setting.

You also use the Memory control panel to turn on virtual memory, if your Mac can handle it. All the Macs that are manufactured nowadays can, but you may have one of the older ones. If your Mac can't handle virtual memory, you won't see a panel for it). You can also choose how much of your hard disk can be used for virtual memory. The Memory control panel is preset to use the same amount of virtual memory as you have RAM, and it's recommended that you leave it at that. You'll need to restart for virtual memory to take effect.

▶ **Tip:** *If you've got a Mac that can handle these special memory features, you've also got a Special Features booklet that explains more about them.*

What virtual memory means is that you get (in effect) a lot more RAM (random-access memory) than you pay for. RAM's what determines how many programs you can run at the same time, how many documents you can have open, that sort of thing.

To see how much RAM you have, choose About This

Macintosh from the Apple menu. You'll also see how much RAM each program you're running is using and how much is left for running other programs.

With virtual memory, System 7 sets aside a certain amount of storage space on your hard disk and uses it as though it were memory. In effect, this increases the amount of RAM that's available to you, even though it doesn't really increase the real RAM. Virtual memory is most effective when you want to work on a bunch of programs at once or work with a really huge document.

About This Macintosh

Macintosh II

System Software 7.1b4
© Apple Computer, Inc. 1983-1992

Total Memory :	8,192K	**Largest Unused Block :** 6,041K
System Software	1,933K	
TeachText	192K	

You can also turn on 32-bit addressing in the Memory control panel, if your computer can handle it (if it can't, you won't see that option). What this does is let your Mac address very large amounts of RAM—much greater than 8 Mb.

Networking Control Panels

System 7 has so many new network features that there's a whole chapter, called "Netiquette," about it. There are three control panels that are for networking—Users & Groups, File Sharing Monitor, and Sharing Setup. You'll find more about them in the Netiquette chapter.

File Sharing Monitor

Sharing Setup

Users & Groups

Which Control Panel for What?

To open a control panel	Choose Control Panels from the Apple menu and then double-click on a control panel; or double-click on a control panel icon in the Control Panels folder; or double-click on the control panel alias in the Apple Menu Items folder and pick a control panel
To change the desktop pattern and color, set the blink rate for menus and the insertion point	Use the General Controls control panel
Set the date and time	Use the General Controls control panel or the Alarm Clock desk accessory. In System 7.1, use the Date & Time control panel to change the formats.
Change the font used in Finder windows, align icons, pick information for list views, and change the size of small icons	Use the Views control panel
Set text and colors used in the Label menu	Use the Labels control panel
Change the beep	Use the Sound control panel
Add sounds	Drag them into your System Folder, in the System file
Set the disk used for startup	Use the Startup Disk control panel
Choose a color or highlighting and window borders	Use the Color control panel

Change the number of shades of gray or colors, set the main monitor	Use the Monitors control panel
Change the "feel" of the mouse	Use the Mouse control panel
Change the double-click speed	Use the Mouse control panel
Set the key repeat, pick a different keyboard layout, set a key delay rate	Use the Mouse control panel
Use keys instead of the mouse	Use the Easy Access control panel
Set the local time, find cities, and check the time difference between them	Use the Map control panel
Change the disk cache, use virtual memory or 32-bit addressing	Use the Memory control panel
Identify yourself and your Mac on a network and turn file sharing on and off	Use the Sharing Setup control panel
Register users and groups	Use the Users & Groups control panel
See which items you're sharing and who's using them	Use the File Sharing Monitor control panel

Fonts and Printing

System 7 comes with TrueType fonts. These are outline fonts that can be scaled to any size and will still look good on your screen and in your printed document, too. Outline fonts are different from the bitmapped, fixed-size fonts that were used as screen fonts in earlier systems. Those would look on the screen like they had jagged edges if you hadn't installed screen fonts for every single point size you used, and installing these took up a lot of room and a lot of time. You had to use Font/DA Mover to do it, and nobody—well, hardly anybody—liked using *that* little utility.

Somebody
Somebody

TrueType fonts are stored as mathematical definitions, and when you ask for a character in a different point size, the system just goes to the font cookbook and takes the recipe for that letter, enlarges it, and fills it up with dots. If you don't have TrueType fonts installed, the Mac will take a fixed size and distort it to the size you asked for.

You don't have to install separate fonts for what you see on the screen and what the printer prints, like you did before. You don't have to use Font/DA Mover, either. You can just drag a font's icon to the System Folder, and the Mac will figure out where to store it. How tidy.

Once you've got a TrueType font in your System file, you'll see that there isn't any point size listed next to it (in System 7 you can open your System file by double-clicking on it). That's because these fonts can be scaled to whatever size you like.

TrueType Fonts

◀ **Tip:** *The fonts you already have will work with System 7, too.*

◀ **Tip:** *Don't confuse outline fonts with* outline style.

◀ **Tip:** *With TrueType fonts, there aren't separate printer and screen fonts.*

▶ **Tip:** *The other neat thing about TrueType fonts is that non-PostScript printers can use them, too.*

How can you tell the difference? TrueType font icons look different. Also, they don't show a size in their name,

Avant Garde 10 Helvetica

and fixed-size fonts do. And if you look on your Font menu in a program, you'll see that *all* the point sizes are outlined if you're using a TrueType font. (Otherwise just the sizes that reproduce best are outlined.)

▶ **Tip:** *If your program can handle it (PageMaker and Quark Xpress can), you can condense and expand TrueType fonts for neat effects.*

You can buy more TrueType fonts, but the fonts you have will also work with System 7. In fact, when you choose a font, the Mac first looks to see if you have it as a fixed-size font and uses that if you do. If it doesn't find a fixed-size font, it cooks up a TrueType font in the size you asked for.

Installing Fonts

Futura   FuturBol

Font suitcase   Printer font

▶ **Tip:** *In System 7.0, fonts go into your System file, inside the System Folder. In System 7.1, they go into a Fonts folder inside the System Folder.*

Well, the world won't convert to TrueType fonts overnight, so the fixed-size fonts will still be around for a long time to come. To install one of these in System 7.0, open the suitcase that contains the font and drag its icon into your System Folder. In System 7.1, you can just drag the whole suitcase icon to your System Folder to install all the fonts in it. If you don't want all of them, drag each size that you want to be able to use as a fixed-size font. Drag the printer fonts, too (if there are any; PostScript fonts have separate printer fonts). Printer fonts will be put in the Extensions folder inside the System Folder.

The TrueType fonts look great on the screen, with no distortion, but one word of warning: if you delete your old fixed-size fonts to use just TrueType fonts, the documents that you created with the fixed-size fonts will reformat slightly, and line breaks may be different. In most documents this doesn't matter, though. But if your document has critical line breaks, test print it with TrueType fonts.

System 7 comes with these fonts, both in TrueType and in some fixed sizes (some of them are on the More Tidbits disk):

System 7 Fonts

> Chicago
> Courier
> Geneva
> Helvetica
> Monaco
> New York
> Symbol
> Times

◀ **Tip:** *Geneva is the font that's used in Finder windows. You can change it to another font by using the Views control panel.*

Times is very like New York, Geneva is similar to Helvetica, and Courier is kind of like Monaco. Chicago is the font that's used in menus.

◀ **Tip:** *To see a sample of what a font looks like, double-click on its icon in the System file, or, in System 7.1, in the Fonts folder inside the System Folder. You'll see several sizes of samples for TrueType fonts, but only one size for non-TrueType fonts.*

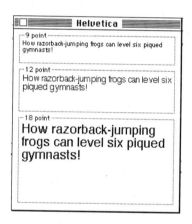

You may be wondering why Apple provides fixed-size fonts as well as True Type fonts with System 7. I wondered, too. The answer is that in the small sizes, like 9 points, the fixed-size hand-manipulated fonts really look better on the screen than the TrueType fonts that are cooked up by the computer. So, to give you the best of both worlds, they give you both kinds of fonts.

Before System 7, a rule of thumb was that fonts that were named for cities (like New York and Chicago) looked best on ImageWriters and fonts that had other names (like

City-Named Fonts

Tip: *Before you buy a new font, look at a sample of it. You may already have a font that's very similar, because only font names can be copyrighted, not the fonts themselves.*

Times and Helvetica) were best on LaserWriters. That distinction is no longer true with TrueType fonts. Any of them will look its best on whatever printer you've got. But your old fixed-size fonts—well, better stick to city-named fonts on ImageWriters and the other-named fonts on LaserWriters. Check the font's icon or see how it's listed in your System file if you want to be sure whether a font is TrueType or fixed size (TrueType fonts won't have a size listed next to them).

Menu Confusion

Tip: *If you've been using Adobe Type Manager, you'll be glad to hear that it will still work with your fonts.*

Tip: *If you've got any of these styled screen fonts, don't apply more styles to them! Don't choose bold for B Helvetica Bold, for example.*

Some fonts that you buy, especially from Adobe, come with separate screen fonts for different styles of type, like italics and bold. If you've got any of these, they may be listed on your Fonts menu in strange ways, like B Times Bold and I Times Italic, and (my favorite) I Korinna KursivRegular. This can make your Font menu very confusing to work with, because members of the same font family will be listed all over the place. It'll be good news to know that System 7 doesn't treat TrueType fonts this way. To give a TrueType font a style, like bold or italics, just apply the style to it.

However, if you're stuck with a font menu that looks really strange, all filled up with your fixed-size fonts, you can get a program like Suitcase II (from Fifth Generation, 800-873-4384) that will let you place styles under a single family name. Or you can get Adobe Type Reunion, an INIT that automatically fixes up your font menus for you (Adobe Systems, 800-344-8335).

Proportional Fonts

One other thing you should know about fonts—all fonts, not just the new TrueType fonts—is that they're either proportional or nonproportional. In a proportional font (which most of them are, except Courier or Monaco), each character takes up a different amount of space, just enough to make it look nice. For example, an *i* takes up a lot less room than an *m*. In a nonproportional font, each character, no matter what it is, occupies the same amount of space. The only reasons I can think of for using a nonproportional font are if you want your printed material to look like a typewriter did it, or if you need to align columns of numbers and letters so that they all are exactly equal.

```
This is Courier, a nonproportional font.
```

This is Times, a proportional font.

Serif and Sans Serif Fonts

As long as we're on the subject of font basics, you should *also* know that there are two basic types of fonts, as far as the typesetting world's concerned. Serif fonts are those that have the little squiggles at the ends of the letters, like the New Baskerville that's used for the text you're reading. Sans serif fonts don't have the little squiggles, like the Futura Bold in the headings in this book. Purists say that sans serif is hard to read for long periods at a time, and so you shouldn't use them for long stretches of text. I agree.

Font Sizes

There's *one more* important thing to know about fonts, and that is they're not all the same size, even if you think they ought to be.

This is an example of 10-point Helvetica.

This is an example of 10-point Bookman.

Why is this? Well, point sizes refer to character height, not width, that's why.

◀ **Tip:** *You can just do your work with a size of type that's easy to read on the screen and then switch to a smaller font before you print the document. Or you can use CloseView, which comes with System 7 (see Chapter 8).*

Special Characters

All fonts have different special characters hidden in them, and some have more than others. To see what's in a font, use the Key Caps desk accessory in the Apple menu. (You need to have the Key Caps icon in your Apple Menu Items folder to use this desk accessory.)

Once you've opened Key Caps, you'll see an outline of your keyboard showing the keys that are available in the font you're using. To see the characters in a different font, pull down the Key Caps menu and choose another one.

Key Caps

```
▤☐ ▤▤▤▤▤▤▤▤▤▤▤▤ Key Caps ▤▤▤▤▤▤▤▤▤
 ┌─────────────────────────────────────┐
 │ see sample here                     │
 └─────────────────────────────────────┘
 `  1  2  3  4  5  6  7  8  9  0  -  =      ☐  =  /  *
   q  w  e  r  t  y  u  i  o  p  [  ]  \     7  8  9  -
    a  s  d  f  g  h  j  k  l  ;  '          4  5  6  +
      z  x  c  v  b  n  m  ,  .  /           1  2  3
                  ☐                          0     .  ☐
```

Tip: *In System 7.1, you can combine font suitcases by dragging and dropping them onto each other.*

Press Shift to see the uppercase characters. Now, here's how to see the secret characters: press the Option key. Voila! You can press Shift-Option and see if there are any more.

Here are some of the special secret characters that are the same in almost all fonts:

Option-1	¡
Option-2	™
Option-3	£
Option-4	¢
Option-5	∞
Option-6	§
Option-7	¶
Option-8	•
Option-Shift-8	°
Option-;	… (ellipsis)
Option-hyphen	- (en dash)
Option-Shift-hyphen	— (em dash)
Option-[	"
Option-Shift-]	"
Option-]	'
Option-Shift-]	'
Option-c	ç
Option-Shift-c	Ç
Option-Shift-!	⁄ (fraction bar)
Option-r	®
Option-g	©

You'll immediately recognize some of these, but the various dashes may need explaining. The smallest dash of all is the hyphen (-), and you get a hyphen just by pressing the hyphen key. (It's after the 0 key, and the shifted character above it is the underscore.)

An en dash is just a little wider than a hyphen. It's used in ranges of things like dates, times, and page numbers, as in pp. 78–79 and 2000–01.

An em dash is what lots of people call a long dash—it looks like this. You can create one of these on a typewriter by typing two hyphens with no space around them, but it's much more elegant to use a real em dash on a Macintosh.

Typing in Key Caps

You can "type" characters from Key Caps by just clicking on the character you want (it'll appear in the box above the keyboard) or by actually pressing the key or keys that produce that character. You might want to type a word that has a lot of accent marks, for example, and then copy and paste it into the document you're working on. (If you do this, though, you should be using the same font in your document that you chose in Key Caps, or you may get a mess of strange characters!)

You can also just make a note of which keys to press and then click back in your document and type the keys, but the warning about staying in the same font still applies.

Accented Characters

To get an accent mark over a letter, press the Option key with the symbol and then type the letter.

Option- ~	` (grave)
Option-e	´ (acute)
Option-i	^ (circumflex)
Option-n	˜ (tilde)
Option-u	¨ (umlaut)

To create a character with an accent mark, press the Option key and hold it down. You'll see a gray box around the keys that produce the accent marks. Then click on the mark you want to use. You'll see all the characters that use that mark, and you can just click on one of them to put it in the box. This makes typing words like mañana really quick!

Tip: *QuickDraw GX, available with System 7.5, makes all sorts of printing extensions possible that will handle things like kerning, case fractions, and ligatures for you. See Chapter 12.*

Tip: *Some city-named fonts have hidden fun characters like a bunny rabbit. That you can get by pressing Shift-Option-~. So sad: TrueType fonts don't have the fun symbols.*

If you use Key Caps a lot, don't close it. Just click back in your document and keep on typing. Then, when you want a special symbol, you can click on the Application menu icon in the upper-right corner of the screen and choose Key Caps again. It's a little faster than choosing it from the Apple menu, because it's already in memory.

Busted Keyboard? Use Key Caps

And here's one final tip, gained from personal experience: you can use Key Caps to create a character that you can't produce on your keyboard if for some mysterious reason a character on your keyboard fails. (In my case I knew the reason: I have several cats, and one of them expressed his distaste for the amount of time I was spending at the keyboard in a way that those of you with cats will know immediately, and for the rest of you let's just say that Pusser shorted out the 0 and I now have a plastic keyboard cover.) Just copy the character from Key Caps into your document. If you need it a lot, use a macro program to assign it to another key combination.

Selecting a Printer

Your Mac will print on whatever printer you've selected in the Chooser, in the Apple menu. As long as you've connected its cable to the printer or modem port (the one

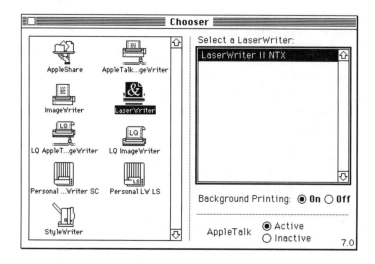

with the phone icon) on the back of your computer and turned it on, of course. If you want to change printers (and they're connected and fired up), you'll need to go to the Chooser and pick a different one.

If you're selecting an ImageWriter, you don't have to pick its name. You just indicate which port it's connected to, the printer port or the modem port.

When you pick a different printer, you'll be asked to go into the Page Setup dialog box (on the File menu) and confirm your options, because each different kind of printer has different options, and a slightly different basic format. Your options may look different, too, because you may be using a later version of a printer driver.

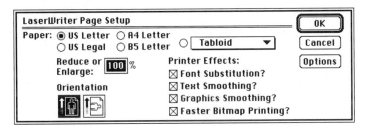

US Letter is standard 8.5 by 11-inch paper. US Legal is 8.5 by 14 inches. A4 Letter is 8.25 by 11.66 inches, a size that's popular in Europe. B5 letter is 9.8 by 7 inches, a popular Japanese size. You can click on the box with the downward-pointing arrow to see a pop-up menu of more choices for page sizes.

Orientation refers to how the image is printed on the paper. If you click on the icon with the horizontal figure, your image will be printed sideways on the page (sometimes called Landscape orientation).

When font substitution is on, you'll get higher-quality text, because the LaserWriter will substitute Times for

New York, Helvetica for Geneva, and Courier for Monaco. Text Smoothing improves the appearance of bitmapped fonts, like Geneva and Chicago (city-named fonts). Graphics Smoothing rounds out any rough edges in your graphics, and Faster Bitmap Printing (you guessed it) speeds up the printing of paint-type (bitmapped) text and graphics, which can get pretty slow.

You can click on Options to get lots more printing options. The ones you see depend on which printer you've selected. (If you don't understand what any of them are for, this is a good time to turn on Balloon Help.) Some printers, like the StyleWriter, don't give you any options other than the ones in the main dialog box.

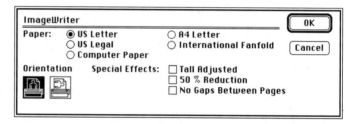

Here's the Page Setup dialog for an ImageWriter, and as you can see, it's quite different from a LaserWriter's. On the ImageWriter, Computer Paper is 15 by 11 inches, and International Fanfold is 8.25 by 12 inches. Choosing Tall Adjusted causes the printer to compensate for graphics that contain circles (normally, they'll print as ovals because of the way the ImageWriter prints), so click that one if you're printing graphics. Choosing 50% Reduction prints your document at half its original size. Choose No Gaps Between Pages if you've also selected Computer Paper.

How do those printer icons (also called **printer drivers**) get in your System Folder? (Actually, they're in the Extensions folder in the System Folder.) The Installer puts them there when you choose Easy Install. Or you may have put them there when you did a custom install. Or you may have just dragged a printer icon into your System Folder when you got a more recent version. Those are all fine ways to install printer drivers.

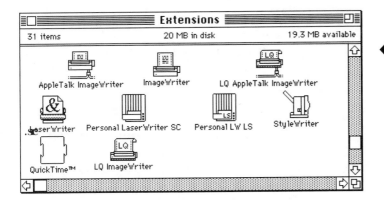

There's an Installer on the system software Printing disk that you can use to install printer drivers without having to install a whole new system.

▶ **Tip:** *If you're using a LaserWriter, be sure that the PrintMonitor icon is in your Extensions folder so that you can print one document while you're working on another.*

If the fonts you want to use are in your System file, you don't have to download them. But there may be times when you want to download a font that you don't use very often and don't want to take up room in your System file.

To download a font to a laser printer, you use the LaserWriter Font Utility, which should be on your Printing disk.

Choose Download Fonts from the File menu. If you don't see the font you want to download, use the dialog box to find the folder that's holding the font. Then select the font and choose Add, or Shift-click to select more than one. When all the fonts you want to download are listed in the box, click Download.

The LaserWriter Font Utility also lets you see which fonts are available on your printer and print samples of them.

Nuking the Startup Page

And it finally lets you easily turn off that pesky startup page that does almost nothing but eat up your paper supply. Choose Toggle Start Page from the Utilities menu.

Downloading Fonts to a Laser Printer

LaserWriter Font Utility

▶ **Tip:** *You can use the LaserWriter Font Utility to initialize a hard disk attached to your LaserWriter, too.*

Restarting the Printer

The LaserWriter Font Utility's menu also lets you restart your printer, which clears its memory. Sometimes restarting your printer is a good idea if you're not getting the results you want.

PostScript Files

You can also use the LaserWriter Font Utility to send PostScript files directly to your printer.

PostScript is a page-description language that specifies exactly how characters and images are to be printed. To create a PostScript file, you have to write PostScript commands that look like this:

```
stringwidth pop
2 div
Right Left sub 2 div
```

and so they're beyond what we can go into here. We'll just say that PostScript lets you create some very fancy graphics effects. Anyway, if you send one of these   files   to your laser printer, you'll be asked for the   name of a file that will save a record of what went on. Normally it's called PostScript Log. If you want to review the PostScript commands that were sent to the printer, you can open this log and see what they were.

Printing in the Finder

Usually, you'll print from within your programs, but there's an express printing route if you're out in the Finder. Just select the documents you want to print and then choose Print from the File menu (or press Command-P). You can choose documents from different

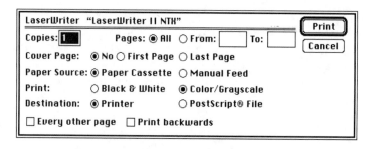

programs, as long as you've got enough memory to have them all in memory at one time, because the Finder automatically starts the programs for you. You'll get a Print dialog box for each document so that you can choose how many copies you want, whether you want a cover page, whether you're using a color printer, and so forth. Again, the Print dialog you see will depend on the printer you've selected in the Chooser, and the choices will be different for different printers, and in different programs.

Printing a Window

With System 7, you get a Print Window command, too (it's on the File menu). This lets you print the contents of the window that's active (has lines in its title bar). If the desktop's being displayed, your choice will be Print Desktop.

Background Printing

If you've got a LaserWriter, you can print documents while you're working on other documents. The trick here is to make sure that the PrintMonitor icon is in your Extensions folder (it's on your Printing system disk if you need to copy it), in the System Folder, and that background printing's checked On in the Chooser.

PrintMonitor

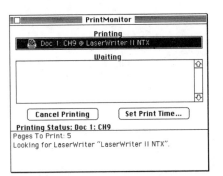

◀ **Tip:** *PrintMonitor's in your Extensions folder. You may want to make an alias of it and keep it in the Apple menu or out on the desktop where you can find it easily.*

If the printer needs your attention while PrintMonitor's handling it, the PrintMonitor icon will flash in the Application menu. If the printer runs out of paper, for instance, you'll see a flashing PrintMonitor icon. Choose Print Monitor in the Application menu to see what's wrong.

(There'll be a diamond next to it indicating that it wants your attention.)

▶ **Tip:** *With QuickDraw GX, there's no Print Monitor. You double-click on a printer icon to see the print queue. See Chapter 12 for more about QuickDraw GX.*

The PrintMonitor window also shows you the documents that are waiting in line, ready to be printed. If you want to cancel one of them, select it and then click the Remove button that appears when you select a document that's waiting.

PrintMonitor also lets you set a print time. This is useful if you're sharing a printer and you want to set your documents to print during the lunch hour, when nobody's around.

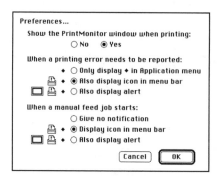

The PrintMonitor menu lets you set preferences for using it, too. You can pick how you want to be altered if any printing problems occur and how you want to be notified when a job that requires hand feeding starts. To set these choices, open PrintMonitor and choose Preferences from its menu at the top of the screen

If you haven't got a LaserWriter, you can get a program called SuperLaserSpool (Fifth Generation Systems, 800-873-4384 that will let you print in the background even with an ImageWriter or a DeskWriter).

Printing the Screen

You can take a snapshot of what's on your Mac's screen, even in color, by holding down the Command, Shift, and 3 keys. You'll hear a click, and a new file called "picture" followed by a number will be created on your startup disk. You can look at these files in TeachText, or in any program that can handle PICT files. Just drag the picture icon over the program's icon and "drop" it.

You can drag to select part of the screen shot in TeachText (in the graphics programs, too) and copy it to the Clipboard or the Scrapbook, so you can paste it into another program. Teach Text doesn't usually have a lot of memory allotted to it, so here's one case where you may want to change its memory size in its Get Info window, if you need to copy large selections.

Printer Problem Tips

All too often, something won't print, or it doesn't print right, and you don't know why. Try these tips.

The most basic one is to make sure the printer's on. If it's a LaserWriter, the green light should be glowing steadily. If it's an ImageWriter, the Select light should be on. Make sure all the cable connections are tight and that there's paper where it ought to be.

Then, go to the Chooser (on the Apple menu) and make sure that the printer's selected. If it's a LaserWriter, make sure its name's selected, too.

As a last resort, turn off the printer, wait a minute, and try printing again.

If your is printing very, very s-l-o-w-l-y, you're probably trying to print graphics, or you're printing a document that has a lot of font changes in it. Either of these can slow your printer way down.

One other thing that can drive you nuts is that you try to print your document from somebody else's computer and find that it looks completely different from the way you had set it up. The most common cause of this is that the font you used isn't in the other person's System file. To fix this, copy the font you used and put it there; then print.

On a network, the most common cause of printing problems is that someone's printing with an outdated printer driver. Maybe it's you. See your system administrator to find out which one everybody's (supposed to be) using.

Printing Shortcuts

Add a new font to your system	TrueType font: drag its icon to your System Folder. Non-TrueType: open the font suitcase and drag the sizes you want to your System Folder. Put the printer fonts in the Extensions folder.
Use special characters	Use the Key Caps desk accessory
Create accented characters	Use the Key Caps desk accessory
Select a printer	Use the Chooser in the Apple menu
Add new printer drivers	Drag their icons to your System Folder's Extensions folder
Download a font to a laser printer	Use the LaserWriter Font Utility
Print from the Finder	Select the documents and choose Print from the File menu (Command-P)
Set a start printing time, change the order of the print queue, etc.	Use PrintMonitor (in the Extensions folder)
Print the active window or the desktop	Choose Print Window or Print Desktop from the File menu
Make an image of the screen that can be printed	Press Command-Shift-3

System Tools

Ever wonder about all the other things there are on those System disks after you've upgraded your new system? There are some neat utilities that some of the rest of us often overlook, or never even know are there. They're not automatically installed when you install System 7.

What you get depends on what medium you got System 7 on and which version of System 7 you're installing.. If you got it on CD-ROM, you'll get a System 6 family for network administrators, a "basic connectivity" set, and even a reference manual in HyperCard. If you got it on 1.4 Mb disks, you'll get a bootable System 7 disk (System 7's too big to fit on an 800K floppy, so you're really starting up with a System 6 system when you install System 7 on your hard disk.). I'm assuming you got it on 800K floppies, which is the basic set. Anyway, in addition to the Install and Printing and Fonts disks, there'll be a Disk Tools disk and two other disks labeled "Tidbits" and "More Tidbits" in the basic set (More Tidbits has some fonts). Here are some of the things you get.

Disk First Aid

Disk First Aid

Disk First Aid is a utility on the Disk Tools disk that you can use to test questionable disks and see if they are good. It also erases (reinitializes) disks and repairs minor damages. It's very simple to use, but it's not as powerful as other disk recovery programs like SUM and the Norton Utilities. But it's free.

How can you tell when to use Disk First Aid? You'll get a message that says a disk is unreadable, or that it's damaged.

▶ **Tip:** *If you can't start your Mac from your hard disk, it's probably not a disk problem but a system software problem. Start with a different disk and reinstall System 7 on your hard disk.*

If you get one of these messages, fire up Disk First Aid. (If you're going to work on your hard disk, start from a floppy.) Choose the disk you want to fix and click Open. If you want to repair the disk if it needs it, choose Repair Automatically from the Options menu before you click Start. Otherwise you can choose to repair the disk later, if Disk First Aid finds any problems.

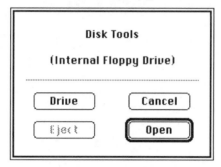

If you get a message that repair can't be completed, Disk First Aid has done all it can. If you have a more sophisticated program like Mac Tools Deluxe or Norton Utilities, try it. If all else fails, you'll have to reinitialize your disk, and you can do this with Disk First Aid. Just choose Erase Disk from the Options menu.

HD SC Setup

Apple HD SC Setup

This utility lets you test your hard disk as well as partition it (divide it into smaller areas). It doesn't repair it like Disk First Aid does.

You can use it on any hard disk that's connected to one of your SCSI ports.

Testing a Hard Disk

The HD SC Setup utility will test your hard disk and tell you whether it's working right. It won't affect any data you've stored on the disk.

To run the test routine, start up your Mac with your Disk Tools disk. Choose the disk you want to test and click Test.

If your hard disk fails the test, it's time to take it in for repair. There's a hardware problem, not a software problem.

Fixing Your Hard Disk

If your hard disk icon doesn't appear when your Mac starts up, the first thing to check is whether the hard disk itself is turned on (if it's an external disk drive). If it is, turn it off and wait 10 seconds or so and then try again. If that doesn't work, restart your Mac from a floppy disk (like the Disk Tools disk) that has a System Folder on it. Then run Setup and choose Update. This should fix the problem without erasing any of the data that's on the hard disk.

Initializing a Hard Disk

Your Mac comes with its hard disk already prepared, ready for you to use. But if you buy another external hard disk, you may need to initialize it to get it ready to use, depending on where you bought it—from a dealer or a mail-order house.

To initialize a hard disk, connect it according to the instructions that came with it. Then start your Mac with the Disk Tools disk that has the HD SC Setup program on it. Then click Drive to search for the hard disk you want to initialize. The number next to SCSI Device: should match the ID number of the disk you're initializing. Your Apple internal hard disk's number is always 0, and an Apple external hard disk's number is always 5. (The number's on the back of an Apple hard disk, and you can change it with your "Macintosh friend," the indispensable straightened-out paper clip. No two SCSI devices should have the same number.) If you haven't initialized the disk before, its

⚠Warning: *This utility won't recognize a non-Apple hard disk. If you have a third-party hard disk, use the formatter that came with it.*

⚠Warning: *Don't do this to a hard disk that has A/UX (Apple Unix) on it. Check the A/UX manual first.*

◀Tip: *You can rename your hard disk. Just select its name in the Finder and type a new one. If you have file sharing turned on, turn it off, or you won't be able to rename the disk.*

name will be Untitled.

When you've located the disk to initialize, click Initialize. When it's done, you can give your hard disk a name, if it didn't have one before.

Partitioning a Hard Disk

If you're planning to divide your hard disk into smaller drives or put another operating system, like A/UX (Apple Unix), on it, you'll need to **partition** your hard disk. It may have come already partitioned, though, especially if you've bought a hard disk with A/UX on it. Check first.

⚠ Warning: *Partitioning a disk destroys everything that's on it. Make a complete backup first, or at least copy off what you want to keep.*

To begin, start your Mac from a floppy disk, like the Disk Tools disk. Then open the HD SC Setup icon (it's on that disk).

Make sure that the disk you're going to partition is the one shown on the right. Then click Partition. You'll see a list of several preset partitions. (If you get a message warning that the disk is in use, click Continue.)

Choose one of the predefined partitioning schemes, or click Custom to do your own. Usually one of these predefined schemes is all you'll need, but it depends on what you're going to be doing. If you think you'll need to do a custom partition, there are details in the *Macintosh Reference* manual that you ought to be familiar with, but we won't go into them here because so few of you will need them.

TeachText

TeachText

▶ Tip: *In System 7.5, SimpleText replaces TeachText. It lets you print, search for words, and change fonts. See Chapter 11.*

TeachText is a tiny little program whose basic purpose seems to be to let you read update notices that Apple ad other vendors put on their software disks. These are normally called Read Mes.

You can't edit a Read Me, but you can print it. You can also create your own to give to others. You'll know they'll be able to read it, because everybody gets TeachText with their system disks.

TeachText only shows one document at a time, so to create a new one, close the one you're looking at and choose New from the File menu.

CloseView is a control panel that comes on your Installer 3 disk. It enlarges the image on the screen. It's not automatically installed when you install System 7, so if you want to use it, get out those system disks and find it; then drag its icon to your System Folder.

CloseView

CloseView

Once it's there, you'll find it in the Control Panels folder.

CloseView
Close View 7.0 ◯ On ◉ Off ⌥⌘O
◉ Black on White / ◯ White on Black — Magnification ◯ On ◉ Off ⌥⌘X
Keyboard Shortcuts ◉ On ◯ Off — 4 × ⌥⌘↑ ⌥⌘↓
⌥ = Option   ⌘ = Command
© 1988–1991, Apple Computer, Inc.   developed by Berkeley Systems, Inc.

After you've turned it on (Option-Command-O turns it on and off, too), a portion of your screen will be enlarged, and you can move that part by moving the pointer. To turn on magnification, press Option-Command-X, and to increase it or decrease it, press Option-Command-Up arrow or Option-Command-Down arrow.

You can also choose to see white on black instead of the usual black on white.

If strange things suddenly appear on your screen after you've put CloseView in your Control Panels folder, you've probably pressed Option-Command-X by mistake and turned on CloseView.

The Apple File Exchange utility (it's on the Install 2 disk) lets you initialize disks for MS-DOS computers (and Apple computers that use ProDOS, if you buy a special translator). It also lets you convert DOS disks to Mac format. To use it, you have to have a 1.4 Mb SuperDrive, or a floppy disk drive that can read disks for both kinds of computers,

Apple File Exchange

Apple File Exchange

or you have to be transferring files via modem or cable between a DOS or ProDOS computer and your Mac.

Using Apple File Exchange for initializing disks is pretty straightforward. You just choose the format you want to initialize the disk in and name the disk. (The only thing odd is that you don't see the disk's icon on your screen later; you just see its name, because the Mac's not really recognizing the DOS disk.)

Converting Files

Apple File Exchange also lets you convert DOS files to Mac files, and vice versa. You can click on Drive until you get the files that you want to translate showing on one side of the window and the folder that you want the translated files to be put in on the other side of the window. Then you just choose which files to translate, pick the kind of translation you want, and click Translate.

⚠ Warning: *DOS allows only eight characters (plus a three-character extension after a period) in a file name. You may get "unexpected results" when the translated files are chopped off to conform to this, and you may wind up with files that are trying to be named the same thing, especially if you convert a bunch of documents with similar names, like Chapter 10, Chapter 11, and so forth.*

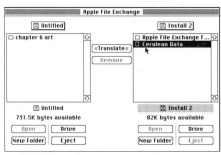

The DCA-RFT/MacWrite translator is for converting MacWrite documents to a format called Document Content Architecture/Revisable Form Text, which is a fancy name for a format that most DOS word processing programs can use.

To see more choices for translating text, choose Text Translation from the menu.

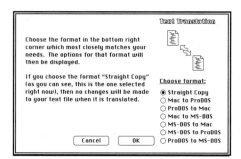

Most word processing programs, like Microsoft Word and WordPerfect, come with built-in programs for converting their documents to other formats.

There are a lot of other options and fine points for using Apple File Exchange, so if you're planning to use this utility a lot, you may want to get more information from Apple. The *Macintosh Reference* manual has more details about it.

◀ **Tip:** *Apple sells a Macintosh PC Exchange program that has many more sophisticated file exchange features. It comes with System 7.5.*

Netiquette

System 7 extends your Macintosh's built-in networking features so that you can share printers and files with other people on a network and decide exactly who gets to see and work with what. As you edit documents, they can be automatically updated for other users on the net. No more swapping disks or printing out "change pages" and then trying to figure out just where they go! (If you've done this before, you'll know what I mean.)

If you're on a network, you can also use programs that are stored on other computers on the net (although strictly speaking, you need a site license to use copyrighted programs on more than one computer). You can use your Mac to send messages to other people on your network, too, just for the fun of it.

Now, you may not be on a network, but System 7 comes with so many networking bells and whistles built into it that I couldn't resist writing this chapter. You can skip it if you aren't working in a networked office, if you aren't interested, or if it doesn't apply. But the day may come when you have two Macintoshes, and then you can have your own network and share printers and files between your Macs.

◀ **Tip:** *If you're not on a network, this chapter's not for you. But if you have two Macs...read on.*

◀ **Tip:** *To use your networking capabilities, you'll need to have installed file sharing software when you installed System 7. If you didn't, you can run the Installer and choose Customize to install it.*

You just plug a LocalTalk connector in your Mac's printer port. It's really easy to set up two or more Macs to talk to each other or to share a printer. All you have to do is buy a LocalTalk Locking Connector Kit from your friendly computer store or mail-order house (or get the PhoneNet substitute, which is cheaper).

What You Need to Net

Tip: *When you connect the computers on your network, the trick is not to leave any unconnected cables at the end of it, and don't complete a circle.*

This kit comes with a cable with two round 8-pin plugs at either end and a connector box. You just plug the cable that comes out of the connector box into your printer port, plug the cable into the other hole in the connector box, and plug the other end of the cable into the other computer's printer port. If you're connecting a whole bunch of Macs and printers, there are diagrams in the kit of how to wire them up.

Tip: *If you're using one of these networks, there are a few other things you need to watch out for. Since they vary from net to net, check with your system administrator to see what your network's quirks are.*

You can also use your Mac on other kinds of networks, like EtherTalk and TokenTalk networks. You'll need to have an expansion card to use these; it goes inside your computer. (If this is the case, you'll probably be working in an office, and hopefully somebody else will take care of the hardware for you.) The software that you need to use these types of networks is on your System disks; all you need to do to install it is choose Customize when you run the Installer and click the type of network you're connecting to.

Using a Network

Tip: *The other computers on the network don't have to be running System 7 to connect to your computer.*

These instructions will get you going, and you can go back and fine-tune things later, like registering users and creating groups and figuring out who gets to see what.

Chooser

The first thing to do to use your network once you're hooked up to it is to go into the Chooser and click the Active button to make AppleTalk active.

File Servers

Tip: *On an EtherTalk or TokenTalk network, you'll need to use the Network control panel first.*

An aside: You'll see "file server" a lot in dialog boxes while you're sharing files. Well, the simplest file server is just a Mac with a hard disk. In some offices there are computers that do nothing but share files, but as far as you're concerned, they're just other Macs. If you're on a network that has file servers, though, check with your system administrator about what their names are (the servers' names, not the administrators'), what your user name is, and so forth, before you go any further.

Network

Naming Your Mac

So that other people on the network can identify your

computer, you have to give it a name. You also need to tell other folks what your name is. The Sharing Setup control panel lets you do this, so close the Chooser and open up your control panels. Double-click on Sharing Setup.

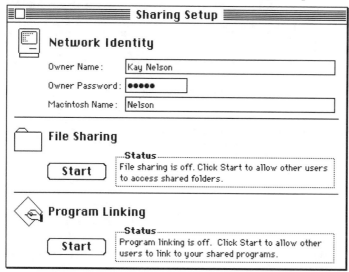

Under Network Identity, the Owner Name is what will appear as your user name on the net, and the Macintosh Name is what appears as the name of your computer in the Chooser when other folks go looking for you to connect to. Fill these out, if they aren't filled out already.

You can also give yourself a password (eight characters max). If you don't, your Mac will gripe at you when you turn file sharing on. See "Password Hints" later for some tips on choosing a password.

◀ Tip: *If you tend to forget your password, register yourself as a user under a different name. (You get to see and change the passwords of your registered users.)*

Sharing Files

The next step is to turn on file sharing. To fire it up, click the Start button under File Sharing.

Now you can close the Sharing Setup control panel and share and folders and disks. Click on the folder you want to share (or on your hard disk icon to share everything that's on it) and then choose Sharing from the File menu. Then click the Share this item and its contents box and set up the access as you want it, or leave it set the way it is and come back to it later.

◀ Tip: *You have to select something first for the Sharing command to appear on the File menu.*

You don't have to share everything with everybody. You can choose who gets to see what. But if you don't uncheck any of the checked boxes, everybody gets to see everything. (You'll see how to set up users and groups later and get some tips about how to restrict access to your computer.)

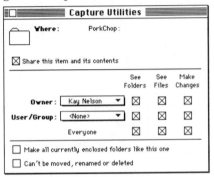

A shared folder looks like this.

Capture Utilities

After you've set things up they way you'd like, close the dialog box. You'll get asked if you want to save the changes you just made, and the right answer is Yes—Save.

And when somebody's accessing it, it looks like this.

Capture Utilities

Now, instead of doing this for each and every folder you want to share, there's a much faster way: Just drag whatever you want to share into that folder.

▶ **Tip:** *Drag whatever you want to share into a shared folder instead of setting up several folders to share.*

You can share folders that are on your hard disk, but you can't share folders that are on a floppy disk—at least not directly. To do this, just drag the folder you want to share from the floppy disk into your shared folder, and the Mac will copy it onto your hard disk.

At the Other End

AppleShare

OK, now you've the user at the other end of the line, and you want to get into the folder that's just been shared. Make sure AppleTalk's active in the Chooser and click the AppleShare icon. You'll then see the other computer (file server) listed. (If there are a lot of them, you can just type the first few letters of the name you're looking for to find it quickly.) Click on it and click OK. You can then choose whether to connect as a guest or as a registered user.

Choose Guest if you're not sure whether you're a regis-

tered user, because normally a guest can always get in unless the guy on the other end has restricted access to his
computer. If you're a registered user, you'll need to supply
the password; guests don't need passwords.

Once you're in, you can pick which items you want to
use. If any are gray, you don't have access to them. You'll
see a list of whatever the other guy has shared. Shift-click
to select more than one.

If you want to connect to this folder or disk *every time you
turn your Mac on,* click the box next to the folder or disk's
name. If you're getting on as a registered user, you can
then choose whether you want to have to enter a password
or not when you start up. Choose Save My Name and Password if you don't want to be bothered with entering a
password each time you start your Mac. On the other
hand, this will give anybody who turns your computer on
access to the network, so you may want to choose Save My
Name Only, just to keep the network safe.

◀ Tip: *Can't get on as a
registered user? Make sure
Allow this user to connect
is checked in the Users &
Groups control panel.
And check to see that
you're using the right
password.*

Copying from One Mac to Another
Once you've accessed a shared folder, you can use what's in
it as though it were really on your desktop. Here's a tip,
though: if you want to copy a program, put it in a folder and

then copy the folder. Otherwise the Mac thinks you just want to share the program without making a copy of it.

To copy items into a shared folder on your own disk instead of moving them, press the Option key and drag them. Remember, a copy takes up room on your disk, but an alias doesn't. So if you want to make a real copy on the other machine and keep the original on your Mac, put a copy in the folder and move it onto the disk at the other end. If you just want to allow someone to *use* something while you're on the network, putting an alias in the shared folder will work just as well.

To copy something from a shared folder onto your own computer, drag the item to your hard disk icon.

> **Tip:** *Set up an alias to connect quickly to your network.*

shared folder alias

Using Aliases on a Network

Once you've gotten set up for file sharing, there's an even faster way to get going the next time you want to use the network. While you're still connected, select the folder or disk icon that you'll want to connect to next time and then choose Make Alias from the File menu. Drag the alias icon to somewhere on the desktop where you can get at it conveniently. You can then go ahead and disconnect from the network (the easy way: Trash the icon of the shared stuff). The next time you want to get on the net, just double-click on the alias.

You can also make aliases of documents or programs that are stored on your network. This is a neat trick because when you open the alias, it'll automatically search for the original and open it, giving you a really fast, automatic way to connect to your network.

> **⚠ Warning:** *If there's already a folder that's being shared, you can't share your whole hard disk. Check the File Sharing Monitor control panel to see what's being shared; then select each shared folder and turn off file sharing for it (with the File menu's Sharing command). Then you can share your whole disk.*

Accessing Your Own Computer

If you want to be able to get at what's on your own computer while you're sitting at someone else's computer in another office, do it this way. Make sure File Sharing is turned on in your Sharing Setup control panel. Then choose the folder that you want to share, or select your hard disk icon if you want to get access to everything on your computer. Then choose Sharing from the File menu. Go to the other computer and use the Chooser to select the name of your computer. Identify yourself as the registered user and give your password. You can then choose the folder or disk on your own computer that you want to work with.

Sneaky trick: You can also make an alias of your shared hard disk and copy it onto a floppy disk. Take the floppy to the other computer and put it in the drive. Double-click on the alias to connect to your own computer.

Disconnecting

When you're done with whatever you wanted to do on the network, you can just drag the network folder or disk icon to the Trash (it won't show up in the Trash, though, so you can't get back on the net that way). Or you can select it and choose Put Away (Command-Y) from the File menu. Or you can just choose Shut Down, and you'll be disconnected automatically when your Mac shuts down.

◀ **Tip:** *Fastest way to disconnect from the network: Trash the icons of the folders or disks you're sharing.*

Registering Users

Normally everybody on the net can see everything you share. If this isn't what you want, you can restrict access to people you choose, either as individuals or as groups. Once you've registered users and groups, you can designate them as lawful lookers into the folders you share.

To register a user, the Users & Groups control panel is the thing to use. You'll see an icon for yourself and a guest. Choose New User from the File menu and type the name of the person you're registering.

◀ **Tip:** *If you're not concerned about the security of your documents, just skip this section.*

◀ **Tip:** *You only have to register each user once. Your Mac will remember.*

Users & Groups

Kay Nelson   <Guest>   New User

Be sure to tell the other guy what name you used here, because that's the name that has to be typed to connect to your computer. The Mac doesn't know about things like nicknames. You may be using Bill for someone who expects his registered name to be Will, Willie, or William.

▶ **Tip:** *Uppercase and lowercase counts in a password. It doesn't matter in an owner or user name.*

Now, double-click the new user's icon and fill out the dialog box with whatever privileges you want this person to have, like assigning a password (better tell the guy what this is, too) and being able to change the password from another computer. If you're expecting to share programs, be sure to check the Program Linking box (you'll see more about this later).

To remove a registered user, trash the icon. To turn off the user's access, uncheck the Allow user to connect box.

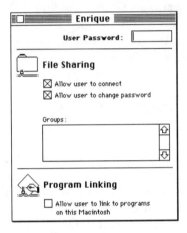

Groups

New Group

▶ **Tip:** *If you need to take somebody out of a group, drag the person's icon to the Trash.*

If you're working in an office, you can set up groups of users and give them access to your files. This is really helpful if you're part of a work group that has to review and update each others' documents from time to time.

To set up a group, go to the Users & Groups control panel, choose New Group from the File menu, name the group, and then drag the icons of all the registered users that you want to have in that group into the group icon (you can Shift-click to select several of them at once). Their icons will remain as registered users, too.

Once you've set up groups, you can restrict access to a folder just to members of that group by using the Sharing command.

There are lots of different ways you can stop people from seeing what's on your computer. You can turn off file sharing, unshare a shared folder by unchecking its Share this item box, or change users' access privileges.

Bottom line: Remember that you have to pick a folder to share and choose Sharing from the File menu before other folks can look into what's on your computer. There's no unrestricted access to everything: *you choose* what others can see. If you don't share a folder, nobody can see what's on your computer anyway.

Turning Off File Sharing

To turn off file sharing so that nobody can use what's on your computer, go to the Sharing Setup control panel and click Stop. You'll be asked for the number of minutes to wait before the water's turned off, so to speak. You can disconnect immediately, but it's good manners to let give the other guys a few minutes to save their work. They'll get a message telling them that your computer is closing down in *x* minutes.

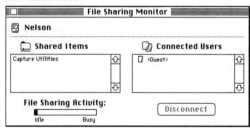

If you want to disconnect just selected users instead of everybody, use the File Sharing Monitor control panel. Click on the name of the guy you want to disconnect, or Shift-click to choose several of them. Then click Disconnect.

No Guests Allowed

You can also prevent anybody from seeing what's on your computer by not allowing guests. To do this, double-click the Guest icon in the Users & Groups control panel and uncheck the Allow Guests to Connect box.

If you don't allow guests, you'll have to register each person you want to give access to.

Ultimate Security

File Sharing Monitor

◀ **Tip:** *You can't Trash the Guest icon.*

Folder Access Privileges

▶ **Tip:** *You'll see these icons under the title bars of shared folders:*

You can't see files

No changes allowed

You can't see folders

You can also change access privileges of folders that you've put into a shared folder. To do this, highlight the folder you want to restrict access to and than choose Sharing from the File menu. Make sure the Make all enclosed folders like this one box is unchecked if you're going to put folders with different access privileges in it.

If you plan to put more folders in it and you want them to be available to the same people with the same access privileges as this folder, check the Make all enclosed folders like this one box.

It may be simpler to set up different folders with different access privileges, give them distinctive names (like the name of the group that gets to use them) and then just drag the icons of what you want to share into those folders instead of having to remember who gets to see which folder inside which folder.

Access Tips

▶ **Tip:** *A tab at the top indicates that you're the owner of this folder:*

untitled folder

can't get in this folder

You won't see this icon on your own computer.

drop folder

Drop folders have to be inside another folder.

You can set up all kinds of restrictions on who gets to see what. Normally everybody gets to see and change everything in a shared folder or disk *if* you're allowing guests to access your Mac and *if* you've selected a folder to share. Here are a few tips you might want to keep in mind:

- To use the same privileges in all the folders inside a folder, check the Make All Folders Like This One box.
- To stop anybody (including you) from renaming, deleting, or moving a folder, check the Can't be Moved box.
- To keep a folder to yourself, uncheck the boxes for User/Group and Everyone, but check the ones for you as Owner.

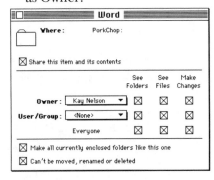

- To share with just selected people or a group, uncheck the Everyone boxes.
- To set up a drop folder to use as a bulletin board so that people can read the files in it but can't change them, uncheck the Make Changes boxes for User/Group and Everyone.
- To set up a private mailbox so that others can send you files but nobody else can see in it but you, uncheck the See Files and See Folders boxes for User/Group and Everyone.

◀ **Tip:** *Set up a message center folder so that you can read messages from the other folks on your net.*

Password Hints

Somebody once said (I think it was Cliff Stoll, the fellow who wrote *The Cuckoo's Egg: Tracking a Spy through the Maze of Computer Espionage*) that you should treat your password like your toothbrush: use it frequently and change it often. If you're really concerned about security, here are a few other tips for password security:

- Don't use a word that's in a dictionary. (Sneaky trick: misspell a word.)
- Use a combination of letters and numbers.
- Don't use your name, your dog's name, your birthday, your license plate number, or anything else that someone who knows you can easily guess.
- Keep your password in a safe place in case you forget it. (Your network administrator should be able to figure your password out if you do.)
- Don't let your Mac supply your password when you start up if you're a registered user and you've chosen a folder or disk to connect to at startup.
- For maximum security, don't let your registered users have the ability to change their own passwords. And give them new passwords every so often. Keep 'em on their toes.

Changing Your Password

To change your password, go to the Sharing Setup control panel and type in a new password. You get to use eight characters, and you can use symbols and numbers, too. Uppercase and lowercase characters are considered to be different characters in a password.

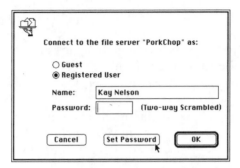

If you're a registered user, you can change your password when you connect to another Mac, unless the Mac's owner hasn't given you this privilege (you can tell by whether the Set Password button is dimmed; if it is, you can't change your password.) Just choose Set Password, type in the password that's valid now, press Tab, and then type the new one (you'll have to retype it to verify it).

Linking Programs

▶ **Tip:** *You don't have to be on a network to link programs.*

Sharing Setup

Users & Groups

System 7 also lets you link programs that are on your computer to other computers on the net, which is great if you're part of a work group. If a program that you have is able to do this, you can use this feature (you'll see Link commands in the program's menus). For example, you might be able to use a spelling checker program with several different programs, or you could perhaps use different spelling dictionaries that are located on different computers on the net. Since these program linking capabilities are specific to whatever program you're using, you'll need to dig out your manual and figure out just what your program can do. As far as System 7's concerned, what you need to do is choose Start in the Program Linking part of the Sharing Setup control panel and then allow remote program linking for guests and registered users in the Users & Groups control panel.

To let everybody on the net link to your programs, use the Users & Groups control panel, double-click the Guest icon, and check the Program Linking box.

You can restrict access to program linking just like you do for sharing files.

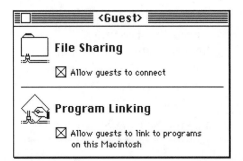

◀ **Tip:** *See Chapter 5 for information about publish and subscribe, which is another handy feature if you're on a network.*

If you don't want everybody to be able to link to your programs, don't allow guests to use program linking. Instead, double-click on their icons and check this box for just those people and groups who need to be able to do it.

◀ **Tip:** *PowerTalk, presented in Chapter 12, is Apple's first step in the Apple Open Collaboration Environment (AOCE).*

Network Shortcuts	**Start using your network, once you're hooked up**	Make AppleTalk active in the Chooser; fill out the Sharing Setup control panel and turn on file sharing; pick a folder to share and choose Sharing from the File menu
	Set your password	Use the Sharing Setup control panel
	Share a folder	Select the folder and choose Sharing from the File menu
	Restrict access to a shared folder	Select the folder and choose Sharing from the File menu
	Register a user	Use the Users & Groups control panel and choose New User; then double-click on the icon
	Set up a group	Use the Users & Groups control panel and choose New Group; then drag the users' icons into the group
	Get into a shared folder or disk	With AppleTalk active, click on AppleShare in the Chooser; click on the file server you want and connect as a guest or registered user; choose the folder or disk you want to get into
	Set a file server up for quick connection	Make an alias of the folder or disk icon you want to connect to and drag it to the desktop; then just double-click on it to connect
	Disconnect from a network	Trash the icon of the shared folder or disk, or choose Shut Down, or select the icon and choose Put Away (Command-Y)
	Share your whole hard disk	Turn off file sharing for each shared folder first

Remove a registered user	Trash his or her icon in the Users & Groups control panel
Set a user's or group's access privileges to a folder	Select the folder and use the File menu's Sharing command
Turn off file sharing	Use the Sharing Setup control panel and click Stop
Disconnect selected users	Use the File Sharing Monitor control panel and click on each user to disconnect
Not allow guests	Uncheck the Allow guests to connect box in the Users & Groups control panel
Change your password	Use the Sharing Setup control panel (you can change it when you log on in the Chooser, too, if you've got that privilege)
Link programs	Choose Start for Program Linking in the Sharing Setup control panel; then allow remote program linking in Users & Groups for guests and registered users

Oh No! (Trouble- shooting)

Just in case you have problems with System 7, here are a few things that can go wrong and how to fix them.

A lot of the repair methods call for you to start from a floppy disk, in case there's something wrong on your hard disk. But System 7's just too big to fit on a regular-sized floppy disk. If you have a SuperDrive or a drive that takes high-density (1.4 Mb) disks, you can make a System 7 emergency floppy startup disk by doing a minimal install, with no printing or file sharing capabilities. (To do this, choose Custom when you run the Installer.) Otherwise, use your Disk Tools or a backup copy of it to restart your Mac, if you have to. It has a System 6 system on it. (If you got System 7 on 1.4 Mb disks, you'll have a System 7 startup disk, because it will fit on one of those big ones.)

Why Is the Apple (or Icon) Flashing?

This one's easy, but it scares a lot of folks. The Apple flashes when the alarm clock goes off. The icon for a program that you're running flashes in the Application menu (at the right end of the menu bar) if the program needs your attention. (Check the menu; the one with the diamond next to it is where the trouble is.) The PrintMonitor icon flashes if PrintMonitor needs your attention.

If you're running PowerTalk, a mailbox icon flashes in the Apple menu bar when mail comes in.

I Can't Throw a File Away!

It's probably locked. Select it and use Get Info (Command-I). Then uncheck the Locked box.

You can't trash a shared folder, either. Choose Sharing from the File menu and turn off sharing first.

I Can't Open a Document!

Check the file's Get Info box and see if it's the same kind as the program you're trying to open it with. Try rebuilding the desktop (hold down the Command and Option keys as you restart your Mac). Try opening the program first and then opening the document from its File menu. Try copying the disk the file is on (if it's on a floppy disk) and then try to open the copy. If the document's on your hard disk, try starting with a floppy and then seeing if you can open the document.

I Get a Bomb Icon!

That's a System error, and it indicates that something's wrong somewhere. Try clicking Restart, if you can. If you can't, try pressing Command-Option-Esc. If everything's frozen up, turn off your Mac and wait at least 10 seconds; then turn it on again. Sometimes—a very few sometimes— you'll have to unplug your Mac to turn it off.

If it bombs again when you start up, try starting with another floppy startup disk, like your Disk Tools disk or a copy of it. If it starts then, you'll know it's a problem on your hard disk. It could be the disk itself, but it's most likely a damaged System file. Try reinstalling your system software. If none of these tricks work, try using Apple HD SC Setup (or your hard disk setup program if you have a non-Apple external hard disk) and reinstall the disk drivers. Then reinstall the system software with the Installer.

▶ **Tip:** *Use the Extensions Manager supplied with Systems 7.1 and 7.5 to selectively turn extensions on and off.*

If you keep bombing from time to time, try this. Restart while you hold down the Shift key. This turns off any extensions that you've added. If everything works fine, try dragging the extensions you've added out of the Extensions folder, put them back in one by one, and restart each time you add one. (Try the one you most recently put in there) You can slowly narrow the choices down to the one that's causing the problem. These control panels sometimes customize your System Folder, which the Mac doesn't always like.

◀ **Tip:** *If you get a bomb, you can also try rebuilding the desktop: restart with the Command and Option keys held down.*

A Happy Mac Icon Appears, but Then I Get a Question Mark. Or my Happy Mac Icon Flashes On and Off.

The simplest solution: try turning off your Mac and then turning on your external hard disk and waiting a minute or so, then turning on your Mac again. If that doesn't work, try starting with a floppy disk that has a System Folder on it. Then run a disk utility program on your hard disk. Your disk may need to be reformatted. You may need to run the Installer and install System 7 on your hard disk again.

I Get a Sad Mac Icon!

Look under the icon. If the first two characters are 0F, it's a software problem; any other characters mean you've got a hardware problem. If it's a software code and you know a guru, try picking his or her brains. If it's a hardware problem, it's repair time.

I Get a "Disk Full" Message When There's Plenty of Room on the Disk.

It's a disk problem and probably fixable. Run a recovery program like Disk First Aid or one of the biggies like the Norton Utilities for Macintosh from Symantec (408-253-9600) or MacTools from Central Point Software (800-277-3873).

What Are These "Disk Full" Messages?

Sometimes you may put so much stuff on a disk that your Finder can't make any changes on it. Eject the disk, if it's a floppy disk, and then put it back in again and delete some stuff from it. (To see how much space is left on a disk, view it by icon or small icon and look just under the title bar in the upper-right corner). Remember to empty the Trash, because System 7 doesn't automatically trash your trash for you.

I Get a "This disk is unreadable" Message When I Put a Floppy Disk in the Drive.

If there's something on the disk that you want to keep, try running Disk First Aid or one of the heavy-duty recovery programs on it. If it's a brand-new disk, this just means that you need to initialize it for use with your Mac.

Before you initialize a disk, check these things: If you've got a PC, too, maybe you're trying to put one of Those disks in your drive. Or you may be putting a high-density disk into an 800K drive. How to tell? The high-density disks have *two* square holes.

My Screen Is Blank!

First, click the mouse. There may be a screen saver program running that blacks out the screen. Then try turning up the brightness control, if there's one on your Mac, it's under the bottom front or right side of the screen. Some Macs have a Brightness control panel that you can use to dim the screen. And make sure the power is on. All too often somebody's turned off the power switch, if you're using a power strip with several sockets.

A Folder (or File) Is Just Gone! It's Nowhere.

Whoops. For this one you'll need to run a recovery program. You've got a disk problem. Try Disk First Aid, and if that doesn't do it, get one of the biggies like MacTools.

My Mac Doesn't Recognize My External Hard Disk!

Make sure it's turned on. Try starting with a floppy disk and reinstall System 7 on your hard disk. If you have more than one hard disk, make sure that each one has a different SCSI number (it's on the back side of the disk drive.) If none of these tricks work, you may have to reinstall your hard disk. If it's an Apple hard disk, use Apple HD SC Setup (see Chapter 8). If it's another brand, you got a manual with it. Use it and the software on the utility disk that your hard disk came with. Before you do any of this, though, just try turning off your computer and waiting a minute, then turning it back on again. This is sort of like looking under your car's hood and closing it up again, but at least with the Mac it clears your computer's memory.

◀ **Tip:** *If all else fails, try resetting your Mac's PRAM (parameter RAM) by holding down Command-Option-pr at startup time. The screen will flash to let you know it's reset. The PRAM contains data about your startup disk as well as the date and time.*

I've Got to Replace My System! Help!

Start your Mac with the Installer disk. Then start the Installer and choose Easy Install (the simplest way) or Customize if you want to choose exactly what software goes on your startup disk (if you're making a startup floppy disk, for example, and you just want minimal system software and no printer drivers).

There's just one catch to this. If the problem is caused by a bad file in your System Folder, reinstalling sometimes won't fix it, because the Installer just updates files. If reinstalling doesn't make the problem go away, try deleting the whole System Folder and then reinstalling. To keep the control panels, fonts, sounds, desk accessories and other things that you've added, copy them into another folder before you delete your System Folder and then reinstall.

◀ **Tip:** *You can't delete the System Folder from the disk that started your Mac. This is another case where you have to start from a floppy first.*

Something Died.

First, check all your cables and power cords. It may just be a loose connection. But don't unplug anything while your Mac is running! You could blow a fuse. Also, don't turn any external devices like hard disks that you've connected to your Mac on or off while it's on. Turn them on first and

▶ **Tip:** *Shut down and turn everything off before you disconnect any cables.*

turn them off last. Also, don't shut your Mac down without choosing Shut Down from the Special menu, so that your Mac's memory is nice and tidy before you hit the power switch.

I Goofed, and I've Got a Bunch of System Folders. Which One Is the Startup Folder?

System Folder

Easy. It's the one with the icon of the Finder on it (view by icon to see it). It's also called the "blessed" folder. Remember, you don't want more than one System Folder per disk.

The Mac's Not Reading My Floppy Disk Drive!

The simplest reason is that it's probably dirty. It's always sucking air in, and whatever sticks to your disks gets left in there, too. Do you let your cat sit on top of your Mac? Don't. I've paid for several expensive Macintosh hairballs that way. You can buy a disk cleaning kit (they're pretty cheap) if you think this might be the problem before taking your computer in for repair.

My Mac Says My Disk Is Damaged!

▶ **Tip:** *Command-Shift-1 will usually eject the disk in the internal floppy drive. Command-Shift-2 will eject the disk in the external floppy drive.*

Don't panic. Eject the disk (restart while you hold the mouse button down, or use your "Macintosh friend," a straightened-out paper clip, if you have to—put it in the little hole to the right of the disk drive and push gently; don't poke it) and see if the metal shutter on the disk is stuck. It gets that way sometimes. Then try reinserting the disk while starting with the Command and Option keys down. If this doesn't work, try Disk First Aid. Or get one of those great disk recovery programs and try it. You should probably have one of those anyway, just for when something will go wrong (not "if").

I'm Getting Messages That There's Not Enough Memory!

Quit some of the programs that you've got running. Remember, hiding windows isn't the same as closing them. You may have a bunch of programs running with their windows hidden. Check your Applications menu (the icon in the upper-right corner of the screen). Restart your Mac if you keep getting this message.

My Mouse Isn't Working!
My Keyboard Isn't Working!

First, check the cables. Make sure the keyboard cord's in the keyboard socket on the back of your computer and ditto for the mouse. Try connecting the mouse to the back of the Mac if it's connected to the keyboard. Check the mouse ball and see if it's stuck. If it is, turn the plastic ring that's holding it, or pop it out (there are two kinds of mouse rings) and clean the rollers inside with a swab and rubbing alcohol. Make sure that there are icons for Keyboard and Mouse in your Control Panels folder. Restart your Mac. Restart it with a different startup disk. If your keyboard is sticking, turn it upside down and tap (don't bang) it on your desk to shake loose whatever may have gotten stuck in there. If the problem is that a key or two's not working, see Chapter 7 for how to use Key Caps to get those characters until you can get the keyboard fixed.

The Pointer on the Screen Is Stuck!

Try pressing Control-Option-Esc and choose Force Quit to close the program you're using. If the pointer works again, save any other documents you were working on; then restart, holding down the Option and Command keys to rebuild the desktop as you restart.

I Can't Save a Document!

This probably isn't a system software problem, but here's how to fix it. Easiest way: Try using Save As instead of Save (maybe the file's locked). Try saving onto a different disk. Check to see that the disk you're saving onto has a closed write-protect hole.

The Mac Says It Can't Load the Finder!

Start your computer with a floppy disk that has a System Folder on it and then copy its Finder into your hard disk's System Folder.

Everything's Getting So S-l-o-w!

If you have virtual memory or file sharing turned on, your Mac may slow down. Another culprit is fragmented files. To defragment them, run a disk utility program like SUM (use SUM Tuneup) or the Norton Utilities if your disk is slowing down.

Help! I Opened an Alias, but Nothing Happened!

The original file that the alias points to may have been deleted. Try selecting the alias and then choosing Get Info. Click Find Original to see if it's still on your disk.

I Can't Change an Icon's Name!

In this case, the usual culprit is that the file has been locked. Select its icon and choosem Get Info from the File menu (Command-I). Then uncheck the Locked box.

Viruses. What Are They? What Should I Do?

Your Mac can catch a virus, just like you, even if you only use shrink-wrapped software. These viruses can erase information, cause system crashes, and damage your disks. If you exchange information this way, it's a good idea to get a virus detection program like Symantec Antivirus for the Macintosh (SAM) or Disinfectant, which is available from most Mac user groups and bulletin boards.

What's New in System 7.5

System 7.5 offers faster speed for copying files, launching and switching applications, and working with menus than earlier versions of System 7. It hasn't really *changed* anything basic, though: if you know how to use System 7 (7.0 or 7.1), you know how to use System 7.5. This new system simply adds things to your basic system. Well, not simply. But that's the next chapter.

With System 7.5 you get all sorts of new control panels and INITs as well as several features that make it easier to work with documents created in DOS/Windows programs. You'll also get a scriptable Finder that lets you automate routine tasks at the desktop level. You can use it as a macro recorder. A new drag and drop feature lets you copy and paste between programs (that is, programs that support this new feature) or store clippings on the desktop.

Several features have also been added to let you make your Mac easier to use if new users have access to it. A hierarchical Apple menu lets you open recently used documents and programs. A flashy new WindowShade "rolls up" windows when you click twice in their title bars, and you can now create Sticky Memos (Post-it notes) on your desktop. Oh, yes, and you'll see the main menu change to provide new menus next to the Special menu, depending on what you're doing, such as working with catalogs in PowerTalk or printing with QuickDraw GX.

A lot of what System 7.5 is about goes on behind the scenes, and a lot of that, such as QuickDraw GX for printing and AppleGuide, the new easy-to-use Help system, will excite developers sooner than the rest of us. Us regular users will see the effects of QuickTime GX and interactive help in new applications.

What You Need

Before you get started with System 7.5, you should know that you'll need a minimum of 4 Mb of RAM to use it (on a Mac Plus and above). If you plan to use QuickDraw GX and PowerTalk (network mail abilities), you'll need 8 Mb of RAM as well as a 68020 or higher processor. If you have a **PowerMac** and you want the whole kit and caboodle, you'll need 16 Mb. Just for System 7.5, you'll need 8 Mb on a PowerMac.

The Good News

The good news is that most of the extensions and INITs that come with System 7.5 can be used independently on earlier system software. So you may not want to install 7.5 but just take what strikes your fancy, or delete utilities you'll never use to save room on your disk. System 7.5 is big. My System Folder after installing one System 7.5 beta was 28,613K before I started to clean it out, but I have a lot of fonts. Blame the fonts.

Installation Tips

So you don't get confused with what's new and what's not, before you install System 7.5, take your System file out of the System Folder. Put it anywhere else. Now rename the System Folder "Old System Folder" and restart. After you've installed System 7.5, you can drag your Fonts folder over from the old system folder, put the extensions and control panels back that you want to keep, and so forth. System 7.5 comes with lots of new toys that you may like better than your old extensions and control panels, so give it a chance and run it for a few hours before you load it down with all sorts of stuff again.

If you haven't already installed System 7.5, be sure to do a Custom Install. That way, you'll avoid installing a lot of stuff you'll never use. After you choose Custom Install, click the triangle at the left of the list to expand it. Then Shift-click to select the things you want to install.

What's In There?

Here's a quick rundown of what you can expect to find in System 7.5. I've grouped the new features together as Basics, New Control Panels, Extensions, PowerBook Stuff, and DOS/Windows Compatibility. We'll cover PowerTalk and QuickDraw GX in the next chapter, because you install those separately anyway.

Basics

At the most basic level, you'll see an improvement in System 7.5's speed for basic operations like copying and starting programs. Everything seems just a little faster.

Drag and Drop

There's also a new feature called Macintosh Drag and Drop that lets you drag selections between documents or to the desktop, where they become **clippings** that you can drag to other documents. The catch is that your applications have to support this feature. The new Scrapbook and Clipboard support it, as well as the Note Pad.

To use drag and drop, all you have to do is select the text or graphics you want to cut or copy; then drag it to the desktop, where it becomes a clipping, or drag it to another open application window.

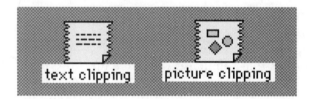

For example, you might want to set up your letterhead as a clipping and then drag and drop it in any document where you need it.

WindowShade

This may be System 7.5's flashiest new feature. A window rolls up when you click in its title bar. Try it. Click twice and watch the window disappear, leaving only the title bar.

This feature is controlled by the WindowShade control panel, where you can set whether you want one, two, or three clicks to activate the window shade.

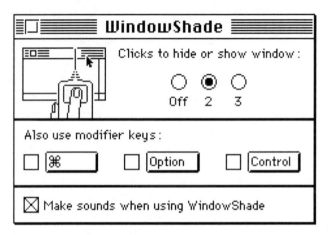

If you don't want clicking to activate the WindowShade feature because you find that you click randomly on title bars, set it to work with a modifier key so you have to Command-click, for example, to roll the window up. Click the Off button to turn the feature completely off if you never use it anyway.

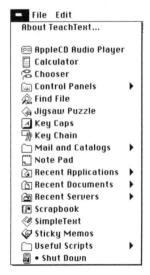

Apple Menu

The Apple menu in System 7.5 is hierarchical—an arrowhead indicates that submenus will come up if you make that choice.

On the Apple menu, new Recent Documents and Recent Applications choices take you to the latest documents you opened or programs you used. This is another very handy feature of System 7.5, although it's been available a while with other utility programs, like NOW Utilities.

Useful Scripts

The Apple menu also lists a few useful pre-built scripts as well as a Shut Down command. Most of the scripts are self-explanatory—like Find Original or Start File Sharing—but a couple of them need some explaining. You can find a

Read Me at the end of the list of useful scripts that explains how to use them.

For example, say that you want to use the Add Alias to Apple Menu script. If you simply select the script, no alias gets made. You need to read the Read Me (or this) beforehand to find out that you need to open the Useful Scripts window in the Finder. Then select the item you want to add to the Apple menu and drag its icon to the Add Alias to Apple menu icon.

Add Alias to Apple Menu
Close Finder Windows
Create Alias Folder
Eject All
Find Original
Hide/Show Folder Sizes
Memos
Memos copy
Monitor 1 bit (B&W)
Monitor 8 bit (256 colors)
Monitor maximum depth
New Item Watcher
Share a Drop Folder
Sound Maximum
Sound Off
Start File Sharing
Stop File Sharing
Sync Folders
untitled folder
Useful Scripts Read Me

SimpleText

SimpleText replaces TeachText. Try it; you'll like it. It holds a lot more. You can choose fonts, sizes, and styles. It has a Go to Page command. You can even record from it or have it speak, if you have the right equipment. Here it is; notice its new menus.

Better Finding

Finally, another improvement on finding! There's a new Find File application that lets you do selective searching all at once. It now appears on the Apple menu as Find

◀ **Tip:** *Press Command-Shift-F to use the old-style Find command. To find again the old way, use Command-Shift-G.*

File, but you can bring it up with Command-F just like the old Find File. Normally you'll see a simple Find File dialog box:

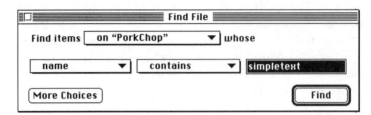

If you click More Choices (and keep on clicking More Choices), you'll get a vast array of ways to search for the exact documents you're looking for. Here I've clicked as many times as More Choices will allow, so you can see all the choices you get.

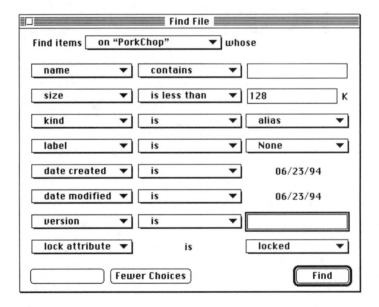

Here's a new twist: You can drag an icon to the Find File dialog box, and its name will appear as what you're looking for. Try it. You can't do this with all icons (like your mailbox, if you're using PowerTalk), but you can with most of them.

The best part is what happens after Find File finds things. You get an easily readable dialog box showing where all the things that were found reside:

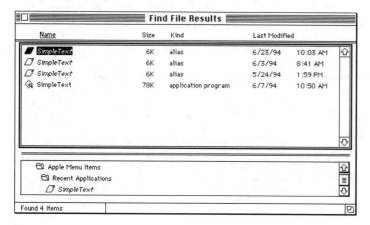

Here's the neatest trick of all: To open the folder where an item is stored, click on the item's name in the lower part of the dialog box. You'll be taken straight to that directory dialog box. To open the item itself, double-click on its name in the upper part of the dialog box. Shift-click to select several items. This really saves time.

And one more tip: To make an alias from a Find File window, Command-drag an item to the desktop. This is too cool. You can also copy from the Find File window if you drag the file to another disk or to the desktop.

Find File is actually an application now. You may be surprised to see it listed on your Applications menu as open. You can Quit it, or you can simply close its windows to quit it.

Sticky Memos

Want Post-it notes on your desktop? System 7.5 has 'em. To use one, choose Sticky Memos from the Apple menu.

To set your preferences for Sticky Memos (color, font, and so forth), click in a note that's formatted as you want it; then choose Use as Default Preferences from Sticky Memos' Edit menu. That's all you have to do. The rest of the notes you create will use that style.

◀ **Tip:** *You can use System 7.5's new drag and drop feature with Sticky Memos to copy text out of a note and make it into a clipping on your desktop. Just select the text and drag it to the desktop or into any program that supports drag and drop.*

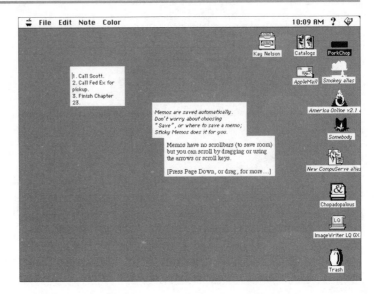

When you close the notes, you'll get a message asking you if you want to see them the next time you start your Mac, so they're great for making to-do lists at the end of the day. You can also choose Use as Default Preferences from the Edit menu and click the Launch at System Startup box to do the same thing.

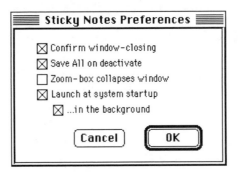

New Scrapbook

You can size System 7.5's new Scrapbook window, for a change. (It has a Size box now.) The Scrapbook also tells you information about what's stored in it, such as the type of graphic and how big it is.

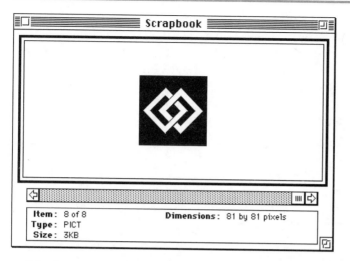

It's drag-and-drop aware, so you can make clippings with it or store clippings in it.

New Note Pad

The Note Pad's been improved, too. For one thing, you can have notes as big as 32K. For another, you can print from it. It even has Find and Go To commands, and you can set font and size preferences for it.

◀ **Tip:** *Try out the animation and sound in the new Note Pad by creating new note (Command-N).*

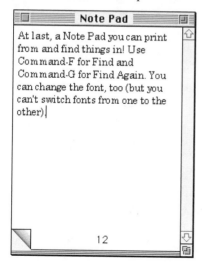

Like the Scrapbook, the new Note Pad supports drag and drop, so you can use it with clippings.

Simplified Basic Operations

If new users have access to your Macintosh, you can use some of the new features in System 7.5 to make it simpler to use and protect your work. For one thing, you can hide the Finder, just like on a Performa. When the Finder's hidden, you stay in your program when you click on the desktop. New users often have trouble with shifting from the Finder to their program when they click on the desktop by mistake, so hiding the Finder makes using the Mac less confusing for them. They can still get to the Finder by choosing it from the Applications menu. To hide the Finder, use the new General Controls panel and uncheck the Show Desktop when in background box.

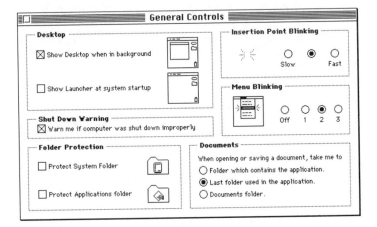

This new General Controls panel also lets you make your Mac work like an easy-to-use Performa by directing all your users' saving to a Documents folder. Whenever they save a document, the Mac automatically opens the Documents folder. That way, beginners can easily find all the documents they create without looking through a series of folders for them. This helps keep your folders from filling up with other folks' work, too.

If you're not setting up your Mac to work for new users, you might want to direct saving to a default folder, either the folder that contains the program you're working in or the last folder you used.

Likewise, you can set up your Mac to use a Launcher, just like a Performa. When you're using this feature and you start your Mac, you'll see a Launcher window listing only the programs and documents you've allowed your users access to.

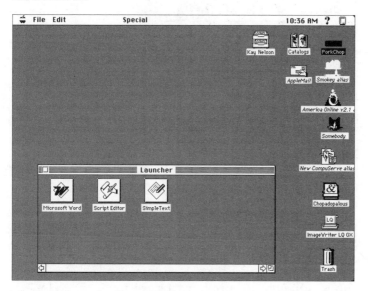

After you check the Show Launcher box in the General Controls panel, you'll see the Launcher the next time you start your Mac. Before you do that, remember to put some items in the Launcher! Drag an alias of whatever you want in the Launcher into the Launcher Items folder inside your System Folder.

One other feature you may want to use if you have new users around is the Applications folder. System 7.5 automatically creates this folder on your startup disk. You can trash it if you don't have any use for it. But if you have new users, you can put applications that you don't want them to use in the Applications folder. Then lock it in the General Controls panel. That way, nobody can put anything else in that folder or take anything out of it.

And one last neat feature of the new General Controls panel is that you can lock your System Folder so that nobody, including you, can add new fonts to your system or remove your favorite startup items without turning off the protection.

▶ **Tip:** *Press Command-? to open Macintosh Guide.*

New Help—Macintosh Guide

System 7.5 comes with a new Help system. To use it, click on the big question mark over by the Applications menu; then choose Macintosh Guide.

Click Topics to see general categories or Index to see key words. Once you're using the Help system, you'll get interactive help for some topics. You'll see circles where you're supposed to click next, or items you're supposed to choose will appear in red. It's a great tool for developers to use to provide step-by-step instructions for carrying out specific complex tasks. You'll probably find it slow for teaching you anything about using the Finder, but then again, if you get stuck, the help is right there.

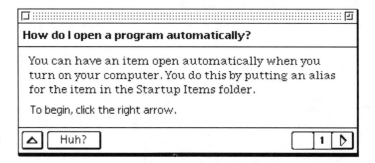

▶ **Tip:** *Try the Huh? button if you need more information about what's going on.*

These Help windows don't get out of your way when you click elsewhere. That's intentional, so you can work your way through a procedure with the instructions still on the screen. Drag the help window by its title bar if it gets in your way. Or use that neat new WindowShade feature to roll it up (click twice in the title bar).

Jigsaw Puzzle

Yep, there's a new puzzle, too. This one is a jigsaw puzzle, complete with sound effects. As usual, you can paste a new picture in it when you get tired of the same old puzzle.

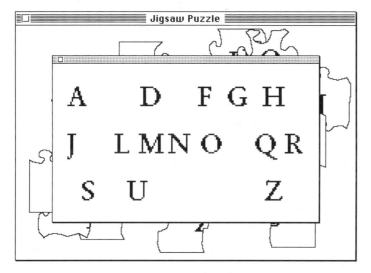

Apple CD Audio Player

If you have a CD-ROM, you can use the new Audio Player on the Apple menu to play audio CDs on it. You'll need headphones or external speakers to make this work.

Easier Printing

Even if you don't install QuickDraw GX, which makes drag-and-drop printing possible, you'll find that Print dialog boxes are much easier to use. Basically, they've just been simplified.

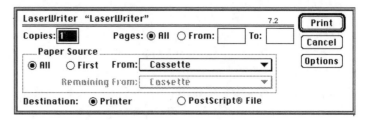

New Control Panels

▶ **Tip:** *If you get a message saying that your Mac can't use a control panel when you double-click on it, just delete it. If you can't use it, why waste space on it?*

System 7.5 comes with all sorts of new control panels. We'll take a look at most of them. When you do an Easy Install, the installer installs 'em all, no matter which type of Mac you have. You'll get the PowerBook and AV stuff along with all the standard control panels, even if you don't have a PowerBook or AV. You may want to go back after the installation and delete some of the control panels you don't need. Double-click on any control panel in question. If you can't use it with your Mac, you'll see a message saying so.

Apple Menu Options

This new control panel lets you customize the way your new Apple menu works, such as specifying how many documents and applications you want it to keep track of, whether to use hierarchical submenus, and so forth.

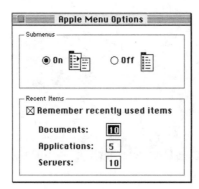

Auto Power On/Off

Auto Power On/Off lets you specify times when you want
your computer to turn on and off, and whether you want
it to restart after a power failure. If you use AppleTalk Remote Access, you'll immediately see a use for this one, so
that you can communicate with your main Macintosh at
selected times while you're away. It doesn't work with all
Macintoshes, though.

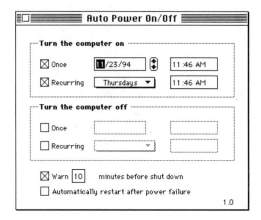

Date & Time

The new Date & Time control panel takes care of Daylight
Savings Time for you. It also keeps track of time changes
when you travel through time zones (if you remember to
tell it). The neat thing about this new control panel is that
you can just tell it a nearby big city, and it figures out
which time zone you're in.

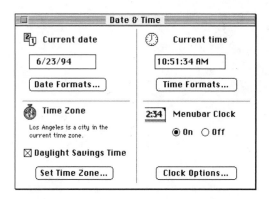

Use the Date & Time control panel to set up how you want the SuperClock, up by the Help menu, to work. You can make it chime and such if you click Clock Options.

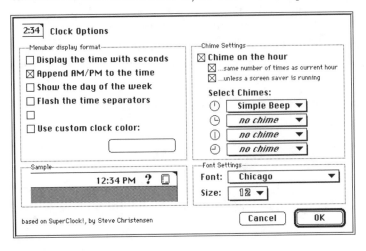

Desktop Patterns

▶ **Tip:** *Double-click on a pattern to select it.*

With System 7.5 you get over 50 different desktop patterns to choose from. If that's not enough, you can create your own in a graphics program and paste it in as a desktop pattern.

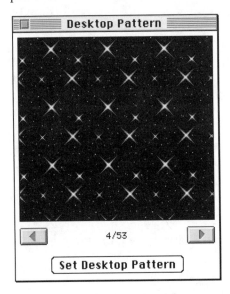

Extensions Manager

This most-useful control panel, which used to be available as shareware, lets you figure out which unruly INIT (sorry, extension) is causing trouble when you start up. It makes troubleshooting (see p. 130) much easier, because you can selectively turn off extensions, or create subsets of extensions. Click its Help button to get help on how to use it.

MacTCP

This one lets you choose a network interface and use the Internet or other UNIX-based networks.

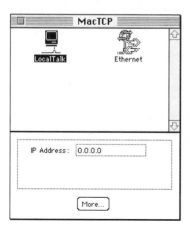

Network

This new control panel lets you change the AppleTalk connection from LocalTalk to EtherTalk, or in general choose a network connection.

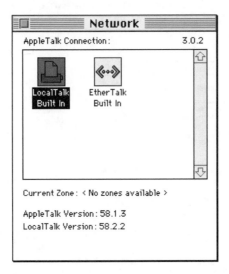

Sound

A new, improved Sound control panel lets you set the alert volume as well as add new alert sounds. To record a new sound, click the Add button or choose Sound In from the drop-down list under Alert Sounds. Choose Volumes from that list to set the volume of your Mac's built-in speakers.

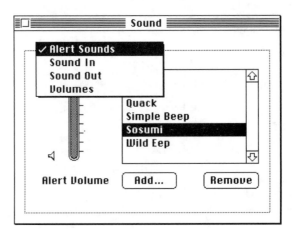

Text

System 7.5 has a new Text control panel that lets you switch to a different language's rules for sorting, using uppercase and lowercase, and so forth.

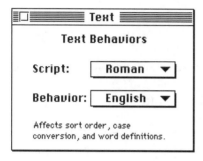

Monitors

A new, improved Monitors control panel makes it easier to work with multiple monitors. To see advanced options, Option-click the Options button.

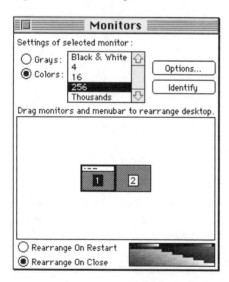

To designate a different monitor as your startup monitor, press Option and drag the happy Mac face that you'll see to the monitor you want to use as the startup monitor.

Extensions   System 7.5 is Extensions City. When you choose Easy Install, the Installer just goes ahead and installs everything,
no matter whether you have a PowerBook, a CD-ROM, a
separate video or what. You can do a custom install to
keep it from installing absolutely everything, or you can go
back and delete extensions you don't want and will never
need. If you're worried about deleting something your
Mac might ask you for someday, copy the extensions onto
a floppy disk. By using a little common sense, you can really clean out that Extensions folder. Here's what (part of)
it looks like as a result of an Easy Install on a Quadra 700.

▶ **Tip:** *You'll see lots of
"Guides" in your
Extensions folder. They're
part of the new
AppleGuide Help system.
If you double-click on
them, you'll just be told
that they're an extension,
but actually they're part of
Help. Don't delete them.*

Name	Size	Kind	Label	Last Modified
EM Extension	7K	system extension	–	Tue, May 24, 1994, 1:59 PM
EvenBetterBusError	7K	system extension	–	Tue, May 24, 1994, 2:15 PM
Programmer Key	7K	system extension	–	Tue, May 24, 1994, 2:15 PM
A/ROSE	72K	system extension	–	Thu, Jun 23, 1994, 10:35 AM
About Help Guide	13K	Apple Guide docum...	–	Tue, May 24, 1994, 2:14 PM
Apple CD-ROM	46K	system extension	–	Fri, Jun 10, 1994, 3:27 PM
Apple Color Printer	325K	Chooser extension	–	Tue, May 24, 1994, 2:01 PM
Apple Guide	527K	system extension	–	Tue, May 24, 1994, 2:14 PM
Apple Photo Access	163K	system extension	–	Tue, May 24, 1994, 1:59 PM
AppleScript™	299K	system extension	–	Tue, May 24, 1994, 1:59 PM
AppleShare	78K	Chooser extension	–	Tue, May 24, 1994, 2:08 PM
AppleTalk ImageWriter	52K	Chooser extension	–	Tue, May 24, 1994, 1:59 PM
AppleTalk Service	20K	PowerTalk extension	–	Tue, May 31, 1994, 8:29 AM
Assistant Toolbox	26K	system extension	–	Tue, May 24, 1994, 1:59 PM
Audio CD Access	13K	system extension	–	Tue, May 24, 1994, 1:59 PM
AudioVision	59K	system extension	–	Tue, May 24, 1994, 2:08 PM
Business Card Templates	20K	PowerTalk template	–	Tue, May 31, 1994, 8:29 AM
Caps Lock	7K	system extension	–	Tue, May 24, 1994, 1:59 PM
Catalogs Extension	410K	system extension	–	Tue, May 31, 1994, 8:29 AM
Clipping Extension	26K	system extension	–	Tue, May 24, 1994, 1:59 PM
Color Picker	124K	system extension	–	Tue, May 24, 1994, 1:59 PM
ColorSync™	78K	system extension	–	Tue, May 24, 1994, 1:59 PM
EtherTalk Phase 2	20K	system extension	–	Tue, May 24, 1994, 2:08 PM
File Sharing Extension	176K	system extension	–	Tue, May 24, 1994, 2:08 PM
File System Extensions	46K	system extension	–	Tue, May 24, 1994, 1:59 PM

You can, of course, delete all the printers and monitors
that you don't have or never plan to use. You can also delete the extensions that have "CD" in their titles if you
don't have a CD-ROM and aren't planning to get one. If
you don't use DOS and Windows disks with your Mac, you
can remove Foreign File Access, ISO 9660 File Access,
High Sierra File Access, the extensions with Microsoft
OLE in their names, and Macintosh Easy Open, as well as
the PC Exchange control panel. If you're not using
PlainTalk (the speech-recognition software), it's OK to delete the Speech Guide Additions. Without an AV system,

you might want to remove the Television Guide Additions, AudioVision, and the Video Guide Additions as well, even though some of these are Apple Guides and part of the Help system.

If you're not part of a network, remove EtherTalk, TokenTalk Phase 2 and TokenTalk Prep; also Network, File Sharing, and anything else that's obviously part of networking. A/ROSE can go unless you're part of a specialized network. DAL can go if you don't access databases. If you have a PowerBook, though, don't remove networking extensions, because the day will come when you'll want to transfer files from your PowerBook to your desktop Mac.

If QuickTime movies don't and never will interest you, delete the extensions with QuickTime in their names. If you don't have a PowerPC, trash the extensions named PowerPC.

PowerBook Stuff

System 7.5 comes with a PowerBook Control Strip that's automatically installed when you install the system on a PowerBook. It's a handy way of resetting controls on your PowerBook without going to the individual control panel that's in charge of the feature you want to change.

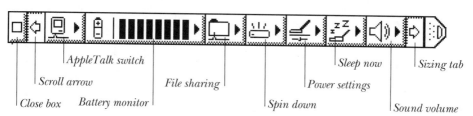

AppleTalk switch *Sleep now* *Sizing tab*

Scroll arrow *File sharing* *Power settings*

Close box *Battery monitor* *Spin down* *Sound volume*

You get icons for turning AppleTalk on and off, a battery indicator that shows your battery's level of charge, how much time is remaining on it and whether it's charging or draining, a File Sharing on/off icon, an icon for setting hard disk spindown, one to set your PowerBook for best battery conservation or fastest speed (the two are mutually exclusive), one to put the PowerBook to sleep with a click of the mouse, one to set the sound volume, and one to shorten or lengthen the Control Strip.

◀ **Tip:** *With System 7.5, you also get a lot of PowerBook control panels. If you don't have a PowerBook, it's perfectly OK to delete them.*

▶ **Tip:** *Keep AppleTalk off unless you're connected to a printer, another Mac, or a network. When AppleTalk is on, your PowerBook constantly polls for activity, using power. Normally you'd have to use the Chooser to turn AppleTalk on and off; use the AppleTalk icon on the Control Strip instead.*

Click the icon on the far left of the Control Strip to reduce it to its smallest size. To open it again module by module, just click and drag on that icon. To move the Control Strip, Option-drag it.

You can customize your Control Strip to add modules or remove those you never use. For example, if you don't use File Sharing, take its icon off the Control Strip to save screen real estate. Open the Control Strip Modules folder inside your System Folder. That's where they're stored.

PowerBook

This control panel lets you set up how your PowerBook uses power. Normally it's set to Easy, so that you can simply choose whether you'd rather conserve battery power or get more speed. Click Custom to get more choices.

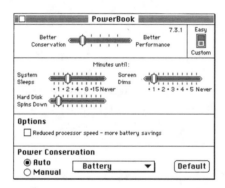

▶ **Tip:** *It's perfectly OK to carry a sleeping PowerBook around.*

To use More Choices, it helps to know a little bit about how the PowerBook works. Its sleep state is a way to save on battery power. When a PowerBook sleeps, its screen goes dim and its hard drive spins down, but what's in RAM is still there. You can use the PowerBook control panel to specify after how many minutes of inactivity you want it to go to sleep.

You can also independently set the time for system sleep to kick in or the screen to dim. Depending on how you work, you may just want to dim the screen and keep the drive spinning so that when you start to work again, you don't have to wait for the drive to spin up.

You can also click the Options box for slower speed—

your PowerBook will run off its battery longer, but at a slower processor speed. If all you're doing is writing in a word processing program, you're not as fast as a slow computer anyway, so go ahead and check this box.

Click Default to reset your PowerBook's power settings to the ones it had originally out of the box.

You may just want to leave Power Conservation set to Auto so that you get top speed when your PowerBook is plugged in and battery conservation when it's not drawing from the AC adapter. It senses when the AC cord is unplugged and switches to the Battery setting for power conservation. On the Battery setting, the screen dims after one minute of inactivity and the system sleeps after two minutes.

Tip: *Ctrl+click on the battery icon in the System 7.5 menu bar to put your PowerBook to deep sleep, with a black screen and no disk activity. You won't have to remember any key combination or hunt for the Control Strip.*

PowerBook Setup

This new control panel lets you select an internal or external modem and set your internal modem to wake up when it's being called. It's a really handy feature, because you can just let your PowerBook go to sleep (even with the lid closed) and still receive a fax when it comes in.

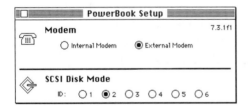

PowerBook Display

The new PowerBook Display control panel lets you turn video mirroring on and off. This feature is used when you've hooked up your PowerBook to an external monitor so that what's on the PowerBook's screen also displays on the other monitor.

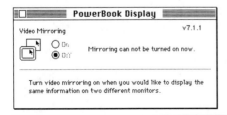

Control Strip

This panel isn't for anything except displaying the Control Strip. Use the Control Strip or the individual control panels to change settings.

Auto Remounter

▶ **Tip:** *Don't overlook the Date & Time control panel, either. It's really handy when you're traveling across time zones with your PowerBook.*

If you have a PowerBook, don't overlook the Auto Remounter.

System 7.5 has a new control panel called Auto Remounter. You can use it to have shared disks automatically remounted when your computer wakes up after sleeping. You can also make it ask you for a password, which is a good idea if you have to leave your PowerBook unattended.

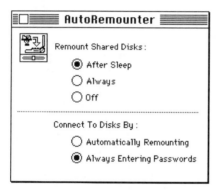

Apple Extras

If you have a PowerBook, look in the folder named Apple Extras, in the Portables folder. That's where you'll find the File Assistant, a Battery Recondition utility (which works only with the newer PowerBook batteries), and other goodies.

The File Assistant

The File Assistant lets you synchronize files and folders so you can freely travel with your PowerBook, do your work, and then make sure that the files on both your desktop machine and your portable are the most recent. You don't have to have a PowerBook to use the File Assistant, though; it will synchronize files between any two disks. If you have more than one hard disk, you can use it to maintain up-to-date files on both of them.

First, decide whether you want to maintain files or folders. It's simplest to maintain folders, because then you don't need to worry about individual files and keeping their names straight. If you use the folder system, each folder can have a different name (although you have to set the File Assistant's Preferences before you can do that), but if you use the file system, the files have to have exactly the same name.

Next, think about how you work. Do you always want the PowerBook version to be the most up-to-date, or do you want the File Assistant to look and see which files are more recent, the ones on your desktop machine or on the PowerBook (or other disk)? You can set up one-way or two-way links. Two-way links are the default, and that's the most flexible method, because the most recent copy is always updated over the older one. If you choose one-way links, you also choose which copy is to be the master. If it changes, the other file will also change when you update your files.

To set up the File Assistant, turn on both computers, start file sharing, and open the File Assistant on each one. Choose Show Setup Window (Command-H) from the Window menu if you don't see the File Assistant Setup window.

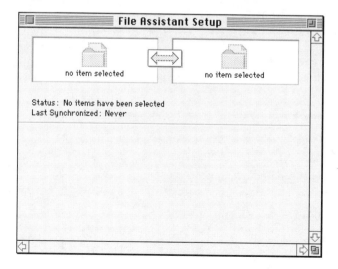

Double-click on the left-hand empty selection box. Then choose the folder you want to link (or the file, but we'll use a folder in this example) and click Select. Do the same for the folder on the right-hand side, choosing the folder on the other computer that you want to link. By default, this sets up a manual two-way link, meaning that files won't be updated between the two folders until you say so, and that the most recent file, no matter which folder it's in, will be used as the master. To set up one-way linking or choose Automatic (so that whenever the File Assistant is running and you mount each disk, the files will be synchronized), use the Synchronize menu.

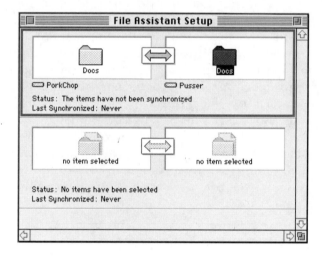

Choose Preferences from the File Assistant's File menu to set up how you want it to behave when it synchronizes your files.

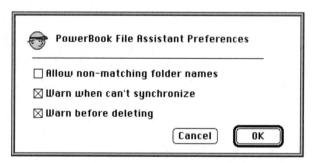

Once you've got your system of shared folders set up the way you want it, you can start the File Assistant and just press Command-G to synchronize your files, unless you've chosen Automatic.

There are a couple of things to watch out for if you're synchronizing files between two computers. First, make sure that their internal clocks are in synch. You won't wind up with the files you think you're getting if one machine is set to yesterday. Be especially careful if you travel across time zones and reset your PowerBook's clock, or you can wind up with a new version of a file that was created "after" (according to the clock) the old one. Then, when you synch the files, you replace the new version with the *old* one.

◀ Tip: *When you're through with a file, lock it by using its Get Info dialog box. That way, it won't get a new modified date stamp if you open it to look at it later, without making any changes.*

◀ Tip: *Files in a directory window aren't updated until you close the window. If you're in the habit of keeping a lot of windows open, this can affect your files' date stamps.*

DOS/Windows Compatibility

If you work with a PC computer, you may need System 7.5's DOS/Windows capabilities. Basically what you get is Macintosh PC Exchange, which you could purchase separately before. But this is a super-useful utility if you work with both types of disks. I do.

With Macintosh PC Exchange installed (and it gets installed automatically), you can format DOS disks, read DOS disks, and open DOS or Windows files with most Mac applications.

To format disks in either Mac or DOS format, choose the Erase Disk command from the Special menu as always. You'll get a dialog box with DOS and Mac choices.

◀ Tip: *I've found that for best results, if you're using a DOS machine as well as a Mac, just format all your disks on the Mac, including your DOS disks. Then you can use the disk on either machine.*

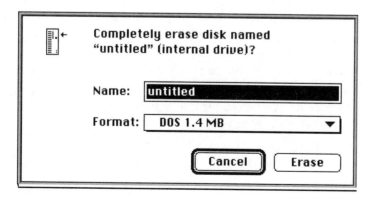

Use the PC Exchange control panel to tell your Mac which program you want it to use to open any of these "foreign" documents. You can also tell it which Mac program to use to open other Mac documents when you don't have the program that originally created the document.

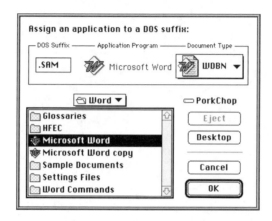

Enter the extension the DOS program uses (PC Exchange calls it a "DOS suffix") and click the program you want to use to open that type of document. For example, documents created by Ami Pro have a .SAM extension. You can choose to have MacWrite II, Microsoft Word, WordPerfect, or WriteNow or another Mac word processor open these documents.

PC Exchange assumes that all documents will be opened as TEXT unless you tell it otherwise. Click on the pop-up list under Document Type to see other types you can assign. For example, if you're assigning documents with a .DOC extension that are coming from WinWord to Word for the Mac, choose WDBN as the document type.

Here are a few more good matches for DOS/Mac assignments:

.WK3, .WK4 (Lotus 1-2-3 spreadsheets)–
Lotus 1-2-3 as type LWKS or Microsoft Excel

.XLS (Excel spreadsheets–
Lotus 1-2-3 or Microsoft Excel as type XLS

.DOC (Word documents)–
Microsoft Word as type WDBN

.PM4 (Windows PageMaker)—
Mac PageMaker as type ALB4

.WK1 (Quattro Pro spreadsheets)—
Claris Resolve, Lotus 1-2-3, Microsoft Excel

.CHP (Ventura Publisher)—
Ventura Publisher as type VHCP

Once you've assigned an extension to a program, double-clicking on the document's icon on your Mac will open it in the Mac program you specified, unless you set up Easy Open to prompt you.

Use the Macintosh Easy Open Setup control panel to set your preferences for how you want translations to work—whether you want to be prompted each time you open a document that comes from a DOS or Windows application, or whether you want it to just go ahead and open the document in the program you specified in the PC Exchange control panel.

Scripting in the Finder

AppleScript lets you create macros in the Finder and in any program that supports AppleScript. A macro, or a script, is simply a sequence of instructions that you specify. You can have a script that brings up your Sticky Memos to remind you of what you need to do the next day, for example.

To install AppleScript if it wasn't installed on your computer already, use the AppleScript Installer. It's in the Apple Extras folder.

You record a script by actually carrying out the procedure while the Script Editor is running, or by writing the procedure in the Scriptable Text Editor, or by doing a combination of both.

◀ **Tip:** *Like most of the rest of System 7.5, you can use AppleScript with System 7.0 or later. You'll need 4 Mb of RAM, though.*

Using the Script Editor

The easy way to create a script is just to use the Script Editor's recorder, or "watch me do it" mode. Everything you do after you turn on the recorder will be recorded. If you make a mistake, or do something that you don't want recorded, don't worry. Just correct the mistake, and that action will be recorded, too. You'll see a flashing icon alternating with the Apple icon in the menu bar to remind you that the recorder's on.

Want a quick fifty-cent tour? To get started, double-click on the Script Editor icon and type a short description of the script you're planning to record. As practice, you can record a Sticky Memo script.

1. In the script window, type Display memos.

▶ **Tip:** *The recorder records only actions that change things. If you move the mouse without clicking or dragging, that action isn't recorded.*

2. Click the Record button.

3. Choose Sticky Memos from the Apple menu.

4. When the Sticky Memos appear, click the Stop button.

You can save a script as an application, which means you don't need to open the Script Editor to run it. You can also save scripts as text files or compiled scripts for opening in the Script Editor. Unless you're into programming, you'll probably save scripts as applications so you can run them by double-clicking on their icons.

5. Press Command-S for Save.

6. Choose Application from the Kind pop-up menu.

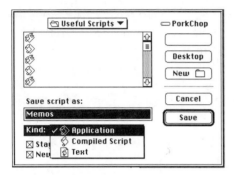

7. Name your script Memos and press Return.

To try running your script, just double-click on its icon. In the startup dialog box that appears, click Run.

Editing Scripts

It's relatively easy to edit scripts because you edit them just as though they were text documents. For example, you might want to change your script so that it opens the Note Pad instead of Sticky Memos. In the Script Editor, choose Open Script from the File menu and open the Memos script. Then change "Sticky Memos" to "Note Pad".

◀ **Tip:** *Open some of the useful scripts that come with System 7.5 to see how they're put together. They're in the Useful Scripts folder in the Apple Extras folder as well as in the Apple Menu Items folder.*

You may notice a Check Syntax button in the Script Editor. It doesn't appear unless you've made changes to a script you recorded. You don't have to worry about that button if all you do is use the recorder to record your actions, because the recorder always knows the correct syntax to use. If you try writing scripts on your own, you'll find the Check Syntax button handy, though. If the script is written correctly, the Script Editor compiles it (turns it into programming language your computer can understand) when you click Check Syntax. If it isn't written right, the first incorrect part is selected so you can find it.

If you're interested in writing scripts from scratch, you'll want to know the words you can use. Every scriptable application has a dictionary. To see its dictionary, choose Open Dictionary from the Script Editor's File menu and pick an application.

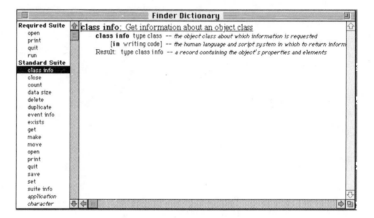

Read the AppleScript Guide that's in the AppleScript folder for more detailed information on writing and formatting scripts.

PowerTalk and QuickDraw GX

PowerTalk is part of what Apple calls "collaborative technology," and it's part of the Apple Open Collaboration Environment (AOCE). I mention that because PowerTalk is the first product based on AOCE, and you'll be hearing more about it. We'll be seeing much more of this sort of thing as the system software evolves. With System 7.5, PowerTalk lets you send and receive AppleTalk mail. With the right third-party programs, you can receive and send e-mail, faxes, and even voice mail from your mailbox. PowerTalk also lets you electronically "sign" your documents so they're guaranteed authentic, no forgeries.

QuickDraw GX is a new way of handling printing that lets you create documents whose fonts travel with them and print by dragging documents to printer icons. You can use it on 68020, 030, and 040 Macintoshes and on PowerMacs. If you don't have one of these, QuickDraw GX won't work.

Either way, installing PowerTalk and/or QuickDraw GX are separate operations from installing your system software. Each comes with its own installer, and you'll need 8 Mb of RAM to use either or both of them. If you have a PowerMac, you'll need 16 Mb of RAM for PowerTalk and QuickDraw GX. That's why we're covering them in this chapter by themselves.

◀ **Tip:** *My basic question was: Now can I get rid of the answering machine? The answer is that you have to buy a program that will let it answer the phone. As of this writing, I don't know of one, but it may be available by the time you read this.*

PowerTalk

You can use PowerTalk if you have several (or even two) Macintoshes connected directly in an AppleTalk network, or if you're part of a more sophisticated PowerShare network with a server. (I have three Macs and a LaserWriter strung together.) See your system administrator for expert advice if you're part of one of these networks. I can tell you how to use it at home or in a small office. That's a nice change from "Don't try this at home," isn't it?

Firing It Up

▶ **Tip:** *You'll need to turn AppleTalk on in the Chooser before you can use PowerTalk.*

PowerTalk comes with its own installer, so you'll install it after you install System 7.5. You'll need 8 Mb of RAM to use PowerTalk.

When it's installed, start setting it up by choosing Unlock Key Chain from the Special menu. The Key Chain basically unlocks and locks your access to the network you're on.

Access Codes

When you first use PowerTalk, you'll be asked for your name and an access code. You'll need to type the access code twice; the second time is to verify that you typed it right the first time, because you don't see the letters on your screen.

Use a code you can remember...but here's how to get around it if you forget it. Open the Preferences folder inside your System Folder and delete the two PowerTalk setup preference files. Then restart and set yourself up with another easy-to-remember access code. You'll have to

▶ **Tip:** *Use the PowerTalk Setup control panel to turn PowerTalk off and on. Changes you make take effect after a restart. Keep it off unless you're using it, because it eats about one Mb of RAM. If you don't see your Mailbox or Catalog icon, PowerTalk is off.*

start your computer with a startup floppy disk to get around the access code (the Disk Tools disk will work as a startup floppy) unless you set up your system as described below.

You'll be asked for the access code each time you start your Macintosh unless you set it up so it doesn't do that. Open the PowerTalk Setup control panel and uncheck the Ask for Key Chain Access Code at startup box.

```
┌─────────────────────────────────────────────────────┐
│▤□           PowerTalk Setup                          │
├─────────────────────────────────────────────────────┤
│  ┌──┐                                                │
│  │  │   Collaboration Services                       │
│  └──┘                                                │
│   ◉ On    ┌─────────────────────────────────────┐    │
│   ○ Off   │ Collaboration Services are presently │   │
│           │ available.                           │   │
│           └─────────────────────────────────────┘    │
│                                                      │
│  ┌──┐    ☐ Lock Key Chain after ┌───┐ minutes of     │
│  │  │                           └───┘ inactivity.    │
│  └──┘    ☐ Ask for Key Chain Access Code at startup. │
│                                                      │
│  ┌──┐    To add services or change your              │
│  │  │    Access Code, open your PowerTalk  ┌────────┐│
│  └──┘    Key Chain.                        │Key Chain…│
│                                            └────────┘│
└─────────────────────────────────────────────────────┘
```

Making a Catalog

The next step is to set yourself up in a catalog. When you install PowerTalk, you get a catalog browser that looks like an open book with a world map on it. This browser holds all the catalogs you have access to, and it also lets you make new catalogs.

To make a catalog, double-click on the Catalogs icon and then choose New Personal Catalog from the Catalogs menu. Your new personal catalog shows up on the desktop, where you can name it whatever you want.

Catalogs

Kay's personal catalog

Making an Information Card

You'll need to make an information card for yourself. Open the PowerTalk folder and select Untitled Card. Type your name as the title.

◀ **Tip:** *For help on PowerTalk, choose PowerTalk Guide from the Help menu.*

Kay Nelson

Then double-click on the card and fill it out.

You can choose Personal Info, Phone Numbers, or Electronic Addresses from the pop-up menu under Business Card and fill those out, too. Be sure to fill out Electronic Addresses so you can get and receive e-mail. When you get to Electronic Addresses, click Add and choose the types of e-mail accounts you have.

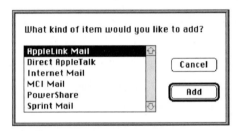

Highlight your name and click Open. Then add your electronic address.

Click the Close button.

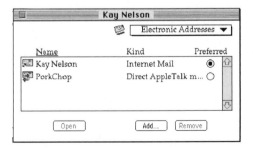

Next, you'll need to make an information card for all the folks you want to send mail to. If you're working in a workgroup, you can probably copy somebody else's catalog that's already been set up and then add a few more names to it.

To make a card for an individual, choose New User from the Catalogs menu; then enter the user's name.

Cards usually go in catalogs, but you can keep cards you frequently use on the desktop.

Sending e-mail via AppleTalk

Before you can send e-mail via AppleTalk to another connected Mac, you'll need to turn file sharing on. There's a canned script under Useful Scripts in the Apple menu that will do it for you.

◀ Tip: *If your catalog icons are dimmed, you need to turn AppleTalk on.*

If you want to send a document that's already been written, find the information card for the person or computer you want to send it to. That card may be in a catalog or on your desktop. Then just drag the document to the user's card.

As usual, you'll be asked if you really, really want to do that. Click OK and wonder why Apple always does this.

At the other end, your recipient hears a beep when the mail comes in, and a flashing In Box appears in the Apple menu. A message appears on the screen saying mail has arrived. The recipient can then go to the Mailbox and double-click on it to read the mail.

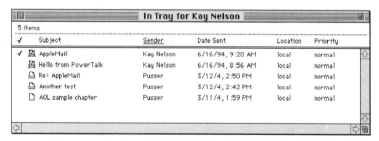

A check mark indicates mail that's been read. You'll see more about reading your own mail in the "Reading Mail" section later.

Sending e-mail via AppleMail

▶ **Tip:** *You can use an already-created letterhead if you choose Letterheads (Command-L) from the File menu. Some of these are pretty flashy. Check 'em out.*

AppleMail is a program that lets you compose and send e-mail. If you haven't written your e-mail message yet, you can use AppleMail to quickly dash it out and fire it off.

Start up AppleMail by double-clicking on it. It's in the PowerTalk folder inside the Apple Extras folder.

Here's a neat trick. If you use AppleMail often, make an alias for it and keep it on your desktop or in your Apple menu. In the Finder, press Command-F to use the new Find File to search for AppleMail; then press Command and drag AppleMail from the upper Find File Results window to your desktop. Instant alias!

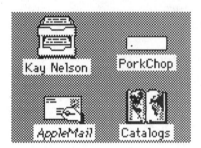

In AppleMail, to create a e-mail message from scratch, press Command-N or choose New from the File menu. Type your message. You can choose different fonts, sizes, and styles; Geneva is the default.

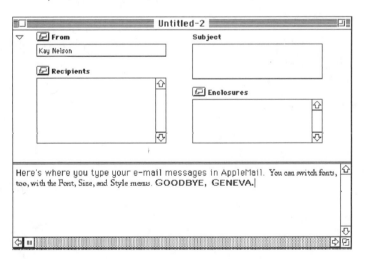

You can read the other letters you've written by pressing Command- – (hyphen) or by choosing Open Next Letter from the Mail menu.

Sending the Letter

You'll have to fill out the Subject and Recipients boxes in the Mailer before you can send your e-mail. Type a subject in the Subject box; then locate the recipient's info card and drag it into the Recipients box. Double-click on the little Recipients icon to go to the Catalog Browser and find cards.

◀ **Tip:** *To add typed-in address to your preferred personal catalog, press Option when you click the To button.*

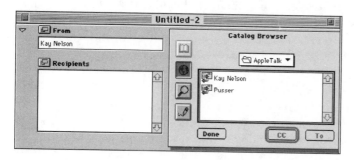

Or, if you know the recipient's address, you can just click the pencil icon, type it into the box, and choose the catalog that it's listed in (more on this below). The fastest way, with no typing, is to click the tiny Recipients icon and then pick a card from your catalogs.

◀ **Tip:** *To delete a recipient, drag the name to the Trash.*

If you're not sure about the recipient's address, click the magnifying glass icon. Now you can search for addresses that match the first few letters that you type. The more you type, the faster PowerTalk can find it.

When you're through addressing, click Done. Press Command-M or choose Send from the Mail menu to send your mail.

Address Mystique

The problem with typing an address is that you have to get it right. If you're addressing mail to a PowerShare user, you use an @symbol before the name of a catalog and : before the name of a folder, like this:

<name>@<catalog>:<folder>:<folder>

For example, if your user is Rachel Anders and her account is in a catalog folder named Marketing Department inside a catalog named Eastern Offices, her address is Rachel Anders@Eastern Offices:Marketing Department.

If you're on a direct AppleTalk network, you can use the computer's name and zone, or leave the zone out entirely if there's only one zone. Pusser is the name of my PowerBook, so I can send mail straight to Pusser. If he were in a zone named Marketing, he'd be Pusser@Marketing.

Internet addresses are a different breed of cat. (Sorry.) If Rachel had an account at Stanford, she'd have an Internet address something like rachel_anders@stanford.edu. Mine is 72000,1176@compuserve.com. There is no Rachel Anders, but you can try sending mail to me if you don't mind waiting a day or two sometimes for a reply.

Sending Copies

▶ **Tip:** *To quickly close the catalogs access panel when you're through addressing mail, just press Esc.*

To send copies of your message to other folks so you don't have to retype it, select their names and click CC when you're in the Catalog Browser. Press Option, and you'll see BCC instead of CC. Click BCC to send a blind copy. BCC copy recipients don't show up anywhere except on the sender's screen.

▶ **Tip:** *More shortcuts: Command-/ expands and collapses the Mailer, and Option-Tab switches between the Mailer and the window where you compose mail.*

The Mailer has built-in shortcuts for sending items as recipients, CCs, and BCCs. To add an address as a recipient, select it and press Return. To add it as a carbon copy (CC), press Shift-Return. To add an item as a BCC, press Shift-Option-Return.

If you need to send mail to all members of a workgroup, it's faster to create a group icon than to send everybody copies individually. In your personal catalog, choose New Group from the Catalogs menu. Give your group a name and drag its members' information cards to it.

Sending Files

If you need to send a file or two along with your message, all you have to do is drag it or them to the Enclosures box. You can have as many as 50 enclosures per message.

Sending Sounds, Images, Movies...

Yep, you can send all kinds of things by AppleMail. If you're planning to send a lot of pictures or sounds, paste them in the Scrapbook or put them in a folder first so you can find them easily. Then just copy and paste.

Saving Letters

You may want to save the letters that you send. You do that just like saving a regular document (press Command-S or choose Save or Save As from the File menu). You'll see the choices Save As Letterhead or Save As Text, too. Saving As Letterhead is a quick way to create a new standard letterhead from the message you've composed.

Setting up AppleMail Preferences

Choose Preferences from AppleMail's Edit menu to set your preferences for the default font and size, whether you want the mailer to expand when you open or create a letter, whether you want the letter to close when you send it, and whether you want the original letter included in the reply (you'll probably hate this because it swells your mail, but some folks will find it useful).

```
AppleMail Preferences

┌─ Sending a Letter ─────────┐   ┌─ Mailer ──────────────────────┐
│                            │   │                               │
│ ☐ Close letter after it    │   │ ☒ Expand mailer when creating │
│   is sent                  │   │   a letter                    │
│   ☐ Issue a reminder to    │   │ ☐ Expand mailer when opening  │
│     save it                │   │   a letter                    │
└────────────────────────────┘   └───────────────────────────────┘

┌─ Replying ─────────────────┐   ┌─ Other ───────────────────────┐
│ ☒ Include original letter  │   │ ☐ Show options when closing   │
│   in reply                 │   │   a letter                    │
│   ○ include entire letter  │   │ Default Font:  [ Geneva  ▼ ]  │
│   ● include selected text  │   │ Default Font Size: [ 12 ]     │
│     only                   │   │                               │
└────────────────────────────┘   └───────────────────────────────┘

                                    [ Cancel ]   [   OK   ]
```

Reading Mail

When you get mail, you'll hear a beep and see a message on the screen. Double-click on your mailbox to read your mail. It will normally appear in the order it's received, but

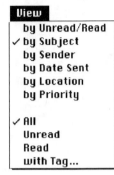

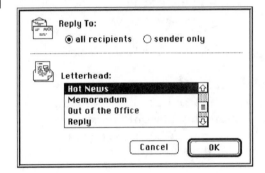

you can change the order items appear in by using the View menu when you're in the mailbox.

For example, if you want messages to be grouped by sender, choose by Sender.

Replying to a Message

To reply to a message, press Command-R or choose Reply from the Mail menu. You'll get a chance to choose who to reply to and what letterhead to use.

▶ **Tip:** *To change the order of items in your In Tray, just click a column heading to sort them by that heading.*

Then, when you click OK you'll be taken to an AppleMail note, where you can compose your reply.

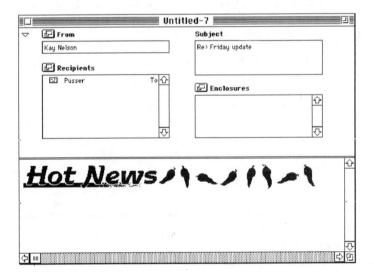

Using Tags

One neat thing to do if you get a lot of mail is display certain messages—those with a particular *tag*. Think of tags as keywords. But tags aren't what you think: words in the subject of a message. Nope, they're special words added via the Mailbox menu and visible in a file's Get Info box. To see a message's tags, select it in your mailbox and choose Get Info from the File menu (Command-I).

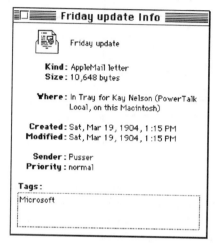

There are two ways to create a tag for a message. One is to use the Mailbox menu in your In Tray and tag mail as it's coming in. Select the message, choose Tag, enter the tag you want your message to have, and click Add (or Remove). Click Done when you've entered all the tags for that message.

The other is to tag messages while you're composing them. To do that, press Command-G when you're in AppleMail, and you'll get a slightly different dialog box.

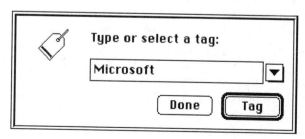

To edit your tags, open the mailbox, choose Preferences from the Mailbox menu, and click Edit under Tags List.

▶ **Tip:** *You can mark mail as Read or Unread to speed up getting through a large volume of mail. Choose these from the Mailbox menu. To set the amount of time items remain in your Out Tray, use the Mailbox Preferences dialog box.*

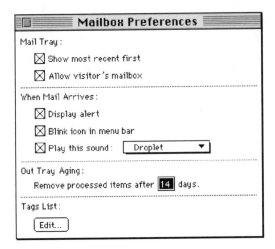

Obviously, if you and other members of your workgroup want to tag your mail, a certain amount of agreement on the key words to use as you send mail back and forth is in order. Once you set up a list of tags, you can choose them from the pop-up list in the View With Tag dialog box.

I might mention that if you display only mail with a certain tag, it's easy to forget that other mail is there. You have to choose All from the View menu to see all your mail again.

Copying Network Mail

Obviously, you have to connect to a network before you can send and receive network mail. Mail you receive over a network isn't automatically copied to your hard disk, though. If it's marked with "remote" in your In Tray, it's still on the server, and if you disconnect from the network, you can't read it. If you're planning to disconnect but you have mail waiting, you can copy it to your hard disk by opening the Mailbox, selecting the remote messages, and choosing Copy Local from the Mailbox menu. Then you're free to disconnect and hit the road.

Just Visiting

You may have noticed an "I'm at..." choice on the Special menu while you're using PowerTalk.

You can have different mail connections at home, at work, or on the road. Choose I'm at..; then pick at work, at home, on the road, or off-line. Then select the connections you want to activate when you connect to a network.

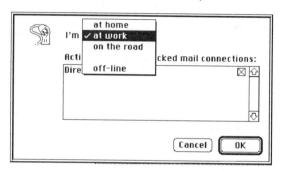

If you choose off-line, you can still compose e-mail. When you send it, it goes into your Out Tray, and when you later connect to a network, it's sent automatically when you reactivate your mail connections.

If you're on a PowerShare network and you're at a different location, you can still get your mail by using a visitor's mailbox on somebody's Mac that's running PowerTalk. You can also allow other folks to get their mail as guests, or visitors, at your computer. To set up a visitor's mailbox, open your mailbox and choose Preferences from the Mailbox menu. Check Allow visitor's mailbox.

▶ **Tip:** *A tiny triangle on the right side of your Out Tray indicates you've been disconnected from the network.*

Then, to get mail at that mailbox, choose Visitor's Mailbox from the Special menu and enter your name and password.

To open your visitor's mailbox, enter your PowerShare password:

PowerShare service: [Choose Catalog...]

Name: [Kay Nelson]

Password: [••••••••]

[ ] [Cancel] [ ]

Visitor's mailboxes are deleted when you shut down or restart your computer.

Digital Signatures

If you're part of a workgroup in which you send documents around for review and approval, you can appreciate PowerTalk's DigiSign utility that lets you electronically "sign" documents so there's no mistake about whether you approved them.

PowerTalk comes with a demonstration Signer that you can try out to see how it works, but your organization has to actually approve your real Signer. You create a request form, print it out, and send it to whoever in your organization has this authority. After you've been approved, you use the DigiSign utility to create your approved Signer.

DigiSign Utility

To get started with the DigiSign utility, double-click on its icon. It's in the PowerTalk folder inside your Apple Extras folder. Then choose DigiSign Utility Help from the Help menu to get specialized help about using it. These Help screens walk you through the process of creating an approval form to get an authenticated Signer.

In the DigiSign utility, press Command-N to create your request form.

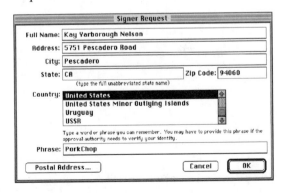

You'll be asked for the code you want to enter as your Signer. It has to be six characters, at least. Choose a code you can remember, because when this thing encrypts, it really encrypts.

After you fill out all the forms and click OK, the utility creates the Signer and Signer Approval request files.

Once you have an approved Signer, all you have to do to sign a document is drag its icon to your Signer icon. Then type your special code in the dialog box that you'll see. You can try dragging a document to the Demonstration Signer to see what happens.

Before you sign a document, be sure that you're through with it, because signing also locks the document. If you try to change a signed document, you invalidate the signature.

◀ **Tip:** *To verify that a document's been signed and not changed, select it, use the Get Info command on it, and click the signature icon.*

QuickDraw GX

Like PowerTalk, installing QuickDraw GX is a separate procedure, and it comes with its own Installer. After it's installed, your printer shows up as an icon on your desktop, and you can drag documents to that icon to print them.

If you double-click on the printer icon, you'll see a print

queue status window where you can control your print jobs.

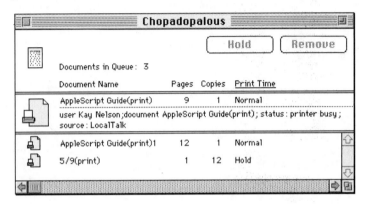

To change the order of a document in the lineup, just drag it to a new location. You can drag it to the Trash to cancel printing, or click Hold to put it on hold.

This replaces Print Monitor, so don't go looking for Print Monitor after you install QuickDraw GX. You can also forget about using the Chooser to switch printers. All you'll use the Chooser for is to install printers: in the Chooser, click on a printer icon and then click Create, and you'll get another printer icon on your desktop. Once you have icons for all your printers, you can transfer documents from one printer to another just by dragging them.

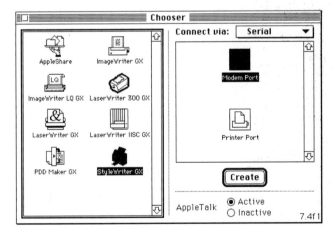

When QuickDraw GX is installed, you'll get a new "magic" Printing menu to the right of the Special menu. It lets you start and stop the print queue, change paper size (choose Input Tray), set a print time (useful for after-hours printing), and things like that.

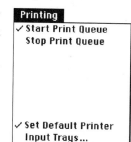

Your default printer is the one with a dark border around it. To switch default printers, choose Set Default Printer from the Printing menu.

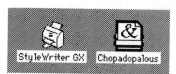

You'll also get simplified Print dialog boxes with new bells and whistles, which of course will vary from program to program. (These are from SimpleText.) They'll let you switch printers without going out to the Chooser.

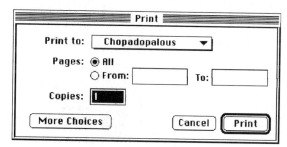

To get more choices, click that button. Then click the Print Time or Paper Match icons to get even more choices.

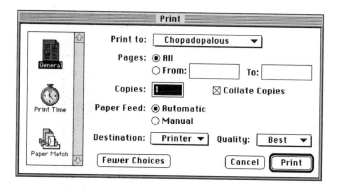

Making a Portable Document

QuickDraw GX also lets you create portable documents whose fonts travel with them. No longer will your readers have to read your text in Geneva if they don't have the exotic font you used. The other guy will see the same fonts you wrote the document in (with QuickDraw GX installed).

In the Chooser (or in a Print dialog box), select PDD Maker GX and click Create. You'll see a new icon on your desktop. Drag the icon of the document to its icon on the desktop. You'll see a Print dialog box where you can pick a paper size and reduce or enlarge the document. Click OK and choose the pages you want to print.

Click Save and give the portable document you're creating a name. Choose whether to include all fonts or only nonstandard fonts.

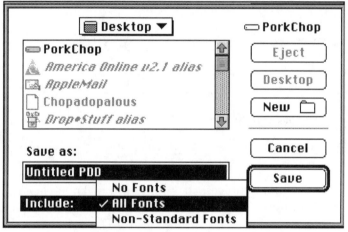

▶ **Tip:** *If you do color printing, there's a new color management system called ColorSynb that lets QuickDraw GX users exchange documents while keeping colors consistent.*

When you click Save, PDD Maker creates a portable document that you can send or give to another person who doesn't have those same fonts. He or she can view the document and print it just like the original. Amazing.

Much of what's new with QuickDraw GX is what's *possible.* It allows developers to put all sorts of new features into their programs, such as watermarks and printing multiple pages on one sheet. They'll be creating new printing extensions that let you choose different types of fractions and special characters or type in languages that read from right to left or left to right, all on the same line.

Installing System 7

Before you install any version of System 7.X, purists say you should back up all your important files before you install . I've never had problems, but it's up to you. But there are a couple of things you should do first.

If you're going from 7.0 or 7.1 to 7.5, here's the easy way to do it. Take your System file out of the System Folder. Rename it "Old System Folder" or something like that and restart. Then install, choosing Custom Install, and install just the components for the equipment you have. Click the little triangle at the left of the list to expand it; then Shift-click to select the things you want to install.

Installer

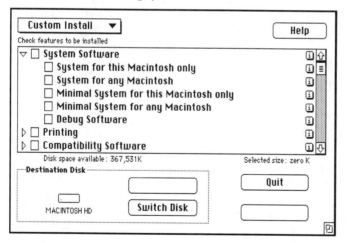

⚠Warning: *Keep in mind that Installers need the same files that they were designed to install. If you're mixing some system disks that are earlier versions of system software with later versions, the Installer probably won't run right.*

◀Tip: *You can use System 7.5's new control panels with System 7.1 or 7.0.*

An Easy Install of System 7.5 will install a lot of stuff you may want to get rid of. See Chapter 11 for some hints about what you might want to delete.

After you've installed System 7.5, you can go back to the Old System Folder and move anything that you really want to keep from it into the new, official, "blessed" System Folder (the one with the little Mac icon on it). System 7.5 has replacement control panels for many extra features that you may be using a substitute for. It comes with SuperClock, for example.

If you're installing from System 6 to System 7, use Font/DA Mover to copy all your non-system fonts out of the System file and into a font suitcase. Don't bother to copy Chicago, Courier, Geneva, Helvetica, New York, Monaco, Symbol, and Times, unless you've purchased these as a complete font family. This will save you hunting for font disks later, when you want to put these fonts back into your new System. Then rename your System Folder "Old System Folder" before you install, and you'll be able to get Fkeys, utilities, or whatever else is in there back later by moving it from the old system folder to the new one. Then go ahead and install.

When you're done, make backups of your Installer disks and the other system disks, just in case something happens to the originals. A couple of backup sets is even safer. And label them! There are too many System 7.X's going around, and it's easy to get confused as to which disk is for which version.

Not Enough Space

If you get a message telling you that there's not enough space to complete the installation, you can either delete some files from the disk (as the message suggests), or you can do a custom install and just put the minimal software on the disk, with no printer drivers and bells and whistles.

Installation Failed?

Very, very rarely you may get a message telling you simply that installation failed. Try dragging all the files from the Installer disk's System Folder onto the icon of your hard disk. Then restart your Mac and check About This Macintosh on the Apple menu to see if the newer system software is there. (The version number's in the upper-right corner.) If that doesn't install the new system, there's probably something wrong with your hard disk, and it's repair time. As a last resort, try using one of your backup Installer disks that hasn't been used before.

Printer Drivers

When you install a new version of your system software, make sure that you update all your printer drivers, too. This is especially important if you're on a network: everybody should be singing from the same printer hymnbook for everything to work OK when you print.

A System 7 Startup Disk

If you have a SuperDrive or a disk drive that will accept high-density (1.4 Mb) disks, you can make a System 7 startup floppy disk. Use the Installer and choose the minimal install option and pick the kind of Macintosh you have. You won't be able to start an SE with a startup floppy that was made for a IIci, for example. You won't be able to print, either.

◀ **Tip:** *If you can't make a System 7 startup disk, you can use your Disk Tools disk, or a backup copy of it, as your emergency startup disk.*

System 6 and System 7

If you're on a network, or if you use more than one Mac, you may run across Macs that still use System 6. You can still use your files and documents on both computers, and in most cases everything will work fine, but there are a couple of things you should know about.

If you're printing on a network—even if it's just two Macs connected to a laser printer—and you use your System 7 Mac to print, you'll get all sorts of complaints from your printer when you try to print from the Mac that has System 6 on it. Put the System 7 printer drivers on the System 6 Mac; they'll work just fine, and there won't be any conflicts. (If you're on a big network, make sure everybody's using the same printer drivers, too, like I said earlier.)

◀ **Tip:** *If you switch systems, use System Picker. It's available on the System 7.1 disks.*

There's an Installer on the Printing disk that you can use to update just your printer divers on your System 6 machines.

Index